american foreign policy
& moral rhetoric

DAVID LITTLE

american foreign policy & moral rhetoric

THE EXAMPLE OF VIETNAM

Published by the Council on Religion and International Affairs

About the Author

David Little is Assistant Professor of Christian Ethics in the Divinity School of Yale University where he is a specialist in historical and social ethics. In 1966 Dr. Little was awarded a Morse Research Fellowship for the study of comparative ethics.

Copyright 1969 by

THE COUNCIL ON RELIGION AND INTERNATIONAL AFFAIRS
170 East 64th Street, New York, N. Y. 10021

Contents

I. AMERICAN FOREIGN POLICY AND
THE TRADITION OF LIBERAL DISILLUSIONMENT

In 1939 Charles A. Beard, that great debunker of American moralism, trained his sarcasm upon a favorite target: Wilsonianism in foreign policy.

> The lines of the Wilsonian creed of World interventionism and adventurism are in substance: Imperialism is bad (well, partly); every nation must have a nice constitutional government, more or less like ours; . . . everything in the world is to be managed as decorously as a Baptist convention presided over by the Honorable Cordell Hull; if not we propose to fight disturbers everywhere (well, nearly everywhere).[1]

[1] From Beard, "Giddy Minds and Foreign Quarrels," *Harper's,* (September, 1939); quoted by Francis I. Loewenheim in his essay "A Legacy of Hope and a Legacy of Doubt: Reflections of the Role of History and Historians in American Foreign Policy Since the 18th Century," which appears in *The Historian and the Diplomat,* ed. Loewenheim (New York, 1967), p. 47. While there may be dangers of oversimplification in Loewenheim's attempt to show the continuity and positive value of the American tradition in foreign policy, it is refreshing to find such a cogent and thoroughly documented defense of that tradition. I am particularly indebted to the persuasive (if too brief) criticism of the views of George Kennan, Walter Lippmann and Hans Morgenthau.

According to Beard, this pious idealistic creed masked a debasing lust for American dominance, particularly economic dominance. But despite his preoccupation with a kind of economic determinism in foreign affairs, Beard typified a broader and very pervasive spirit of liberal disillusionment in the period between the wars, a spirit that has been ably summarized by Professor Robert Osgood: "Strip the cloak of propaganda and ideology off international relations, and the assumption was that one would always find the same old familiar pattern of self-seeking in diplomacy."[2]

Beard and his confreres were not, it must be remembered, morally indifferent or unreservedly cynical. On the contrary. Themselves disillusioned idealists, they were intent upon rooting out and exposing what they believed were precisely the *immoral* consequences of idealism in foreign affairs. It was not simply, for example, that Wilson's lofty rhetoric about opposing aggression and defending self-determination hypocritically cloaked less flattering, but more genuine, national interests. More seriously, such rhetoric provided a warrant for national self-seeking on a scale that could only work disaster for the country in question, as well as for the world at large. In general, the major point of these disillusioned liberals could be reduced to the following maxim: *moralism and idealism in international affairs produce more harm than good*.[3] That is, for the sake of everyone's welfare, the reasons

[2] Robert F. Osgood, *Ideals and Self-Interest in America's Foreign Policy* (Chicago, 1953), p. 369.

[3] For Beard's extensive analysis of this point, see particularly "Moral Obligation in National Interest," ch. VIII of *The Idea of National Interest* (Chicago, 1966; originally published in 1934). As Beard puts it, "objective criteria appear to be lacking, both for the interpretation

or justifications nations give for their behavior ought to stay as close to "real interests" as possible. High-sounding idealistic justifications — like "protecting freedom" or "making the world safe for democracy" — both delude nations as to their real motives and lead to preposterous excursions where success is impossible.

The ghost of liberal disillusionment is very much with us today. Indeed, the attempt to direct, or redirect, foreign policy by means of deflating political rhetoric, and revealing for all to see why the United States government "really" conducts itself as it does, appears to be the consuming passion of many important intellectuals, commentators and senators. By no means do I intend to trivialize the recent observations on foreign policy by people such as Senator Fulbright, Reinhold Niebuhr, or Theodore Draper when I suggest that the basic theme of each is a variation on Beard's theme; the foreign policy rhetoric of the U.S. government masks a lust for dom-

and testing of moral obligation, and for determining 'the true' national interest. Nevertheless, allegedly to realize the precepts of moral obligation in action, all the engines of war, conquest, economic pressure, religious dogma, social control, and political power have been employed" (p. 292).

Actually, Beard claimed that the real problem with an emphasis on moral obligation was that it provided a cover for particular, private interests within the country and did not promote the common, which is to say the real, economic interest of the U.S. As Paul Seabury has pointed out in his helpful volume, *Power, Freedom and Diplomacy* (New York, 1967), Beard "could never free himself from the conviction that the stated national interests of the U.S. government were merely cover-ups for private or selfish motives. Later, during W.W. II, Beard interpreted Roosevelt's interventionist policies in the European war as a conspiracy to keep the New Deal in power and American business interests viable by means of fabricated crisis" (p. 287).

9

inance that is potentially destructive of its real interests, as well as those of the world.

Like so many other critics, Senator Fulbright seeks to look behind the justifications supplied by our government for its various decisions, to ascertain its real motivations. The United States assumes and maintains responsibilities in unlikely places like Vietnam, Fulbright believes, because of "an excess of pride born of power. Power has a way of undermining judgment. . . . The idea of being responsible for the whole world seems to have dazzled us, giving rise to what I call the arrogance of power. . . ."[4] And simply putting Beard's basic point in other language, Fulbright argues that "a man's principal business in foreign policy . . . is to keep his own house in order."[5]

Similarly, Reinhold Niebuhr — his own thoughts on foreign policy so clearly influenced by the liberal disillusionment of the '20's and '30's[6] — intends to strip away the "pretensions" that surround U.S. policy in Vietnam.

The phenomenal expansion of the Vietnam venture . . .

[4] *The Arrogance of Power* (New York, 1966), p. 130.

[5] *Ibid.*, p. 255.

[6] By far the greatest number of references in Chapter 4, "The Morality of Nations," in *Moral Man and Immoral Society* (1932), are to the writings of Walter Millis who, along with Charles Beard and others, exposed in a popularized fashion the "real reasons" for U.S. intervention in World War I. Unlike some of the other more serious and impartial historical inquiries into the origins of W. W. I, Millis' work was intended to bolster the growing isolationism of the period, although he himself departed from his isolationism just before W. W. II. See Osgood, *op. cit.*, pp. 367-68; 400-401. Cf. Loewenheim, *op. cit.*, pp. 42-48, for some harsh judgments regarding the character and impact of works like Millis'.

create[s] the suspicion that our loyalty to Wilsonian international ideas (or in the President's phrase, "Our determination not to desert our principles or our friends") was not powerful enough to motivate this tremendous expenditure of blood and treasure. *Some unconscious and unconfessed motives must have been behind this vast undertaking.*

The most obvious motivating forces must have been the unconscious concern of the people for *the pride and prestige of their imperial nation, and the unconfessed identical concern of our political leaders.*[7]

Finally, Theodore Draper's recent book, significantly entitled *Abuse of Power,* also sets out to reveal what he believes to be the obvious absurdity of the Administration's justification for Vietnam. (Draper's book has received the wholesale endorsement of Reinhold Niebuhr, not to mention former Presidential advisor, Richard Goodwin.) The book abounds with statements like the following: "The idea that the frustration of a Communist bid for power in South Vietnam will be some kind of decisive setback for communism in Southeast Asia . . . is a political fairy tale."[8] Rather, Draper contends, the real explanation for U.S. policy, not only in Vietnam but all over the globe, is "the new worship of power."[9]

We could exhibit many more recent examples of this honorable tradition of liberal debunking in matters of foreign

[7] "Foreign Policy in a New Context," *New Leader* (February 27, 1966), p. 19; italics supplied.

[8] (New York, 1967), p. 114. This is an expansion of two shorter essays by Draper, "The American Crisis," *Commentary* (January, 1967), and "How Not to Negotiate," *New York Review of Books* (May 4, 1967).

[9] *Ibid.,* p. 219.

11

policy, citing Kahin and Lewis' *United States in Vietnam*,[10] Howard Zinn's *Vietnam: The Logic of Withdrawal*,[11] the continuing essays of Hans Morgenthau,[12] the articles of Henry Steele Commager,[13] or the provocative book by Carl Oglesby and Richard Shaull, *Containment and Change*[14] — a book of special interest, in this connection, because at least Oglesby's contribution appears to be a direct extension of the particulars of Beard's economic reductionism. However, further illustrations are unnecessary to indicate something of the greatest interest to us in this essay: the intense *moral* passion with which the critics assail the government's own moral

[10] In recently working through the essays of Richard A. Falk, certainly the most informed and articulate critic of the U.S. legal position in Vietnam, I was appalled to note how much he relies on Kahin and Lewis; see Falk's essays in *The Vietnam War and International Law,* ed. Falk (Princeton, 1968). In my judgment, David Halberstam has properly assessed the Kahin and Lewis volume: "The book would be considerably more valuable if it were more balanced and spent more time describing the conditions that governed the various key decisions." *New York Times Book Review* (April 10, 1967), p. 7. Halberstam's words should be borne in mind by all debunkers of American foreign policy.

[11] See also Zinn, "Vietnam: Setting the Moral Equation," *The Nation* (January 17, 1966). Cf. William Henry Harris, "Morality, Moralism and Vietnam," *Christian Century* (September 22, 1965), for an article that argues that the U.S. government is obviously guilty of moralistic rationalizations in its Vietnam policy.

[12] See Hans J. Morgenthau, *Vietnam and the United States* (Washington, D.C., 1965). Cf. "The Mainsprings of American Foreign Policy —The National Interest vs. Moral Abstractions," *American Political Science Review* (December, 1950).

[13] See, e.g., "How Not to Be a World Power," *New York Times Magazine* (March 12, 1967).

[14] (New York, 1967).

justifications for its action.

Like their predecessors of the '20's and '30's, these present-day critics are not charging the government simply with mistakes in judgment or in argument or with honest miscalculations in difficult questions. No, the government is generally charged with willful or near-willful deception; with more or less deliberately using justifications for policy which are so transparently absurd as to be an obvious "snow job" (in one of Zinn's unflattering characterizations). I call attention here to the wording of the passage from Reinhold Niebuhr quoted above. He claims that one of the "real" reasons for U.S. involvement in Vietnam is the concern for pride and prestige on the part of people and government. But for the people it is an "unconscious" concern. For "our political leaders," on the other hand, the passion for prestige is "unconfessed." This interesting distinction leaves the impression that, for Niebuhr, the Administration is the more blameworthy because it more or less consciously refuses to admit what could, to any perceptive person, be the only possible explanation for U.S. policy in Vietnam. By contrast, the populace at large is driven by motivations of which it is unaware. It would appear, therefore, to bear less responsibility, judging from Niebuhr's phrasing.[15]

Of course, the critical literature — except on the extreme right and left[16] — usually stops well short of accusing our

15 People who will not admit what they know to be true are more contemptible than those who are not aware of what they are doing. Niebuhr (and all the critics) needs to establish some such distinction as this in order to make his condemnation stick.

16 On the Right see, for example, Robert Welch's pamphlet "The Truth About Vietnam": "Does anybody have any doubts as to who is

leaders of cynical and thoroughly deliberate deception. The Administration is more likely to be described as a prisoner of its own moralistic rationalizations, partly unable, although also partly unwilling, to "confess" what truly drives it to do the things it does. But whatever the degree of deliberate deception, the critics are clear that the government is *morally* to blame for employing in the first place its idealistic categories, however much it may actually believe in them. As we have noted, the cardinal maxim of the Beardian tradition is that moralism and idealism in international affairs produce more harm than good.

It is enlightening to examine the place and significance of this maxim in the contemporary discussion of morality in foreign policy. Undoubtedly, the most prominent and respected representative of the tradition of liberal disillusionment in America is George F. Kennan. Kennan's influence upon both the shaping of foreign policy and intelligent reflection about it has been immense. His early career in the foreign service took place during the tumultuous period between the wars when, as we have mentioned, Wilsonian idealism was persistently and gleefully excoriated by men like Charles Beard. The following statements, which epitomize Kennan's point of view, can only be understood against his experience in the '20's and '30's.

I see the most serious fault of our past policy formulation to lie in something that I might call the legalistic-moralistic

really running things in Washington today, or that our actions in Vietnam are being conducted exactly according to Communist plans and wishes?" For writings hardly more circumspect on the Left see, for example, Wilfred G. Burchett, *Vietnam: Inside Story of the Guerrilla War* (New York, 1965).

14

approach to international problems.[17] Let us not assume that the *purposes* of states, as distinct from the methods, are fit subjects for measurement in moral terms. . . .[18] [Instead, he urges, we should] have the modesty to admit that our national interest is all that we are really capable of knowing and understanding, [as well as] the courage to recognize that if our purposes and undertakings here at home are decent ones, unsullied by arrogance or hostility toward other people or delusions of superiority, then the pursuit of our national interest can never fail to be conducive to a better world.[19] [Or, as he said at the Vietnam Hearings,] there are limits to what our duties and our capabilities are, and our first duty is to ourselves.[20]

Taken superficially, as many "hard-headed" moderns have been inclined to take them, these words appear quite unambigously to divorce altogether the consideration of morality from international affairs. They seem to support a sort of modern Machiavellianism. However, these are not the sentiments of a moral cynic. Like Beard and his sympathizers, Kennan has a keen — if not always clear-headed — moral objective. If this is not apparent to his readers it is because of certain serious confusions in his writings which, I shall suggest, also plague others of our contemporaries who stand in the tradition of liberal disillusionment. Before we can hope

17 George F. Kennan, *American Diplomacy, 1900-1950* (New York, 1951), p. 82.

18 *Realities of American Foreign Policy* (Princeton, 1954), pp. 47-48.

19 Kennan, *op. cit.*, p. 88.

20 *Vietnam Hearings,* ed. Sen. J. W. Fulbright (New York, 1966), p. 118; cf. *Realities of American Foreign Policy,* p. 47.

to construct a helpful positive position regarding morals in foreign relations we must, I believe, attempt to clear up some of these difficulties.

Kennan causes confusion when he, like some other realists, asserts the irrelevance of moral values to the purposes of government.[21] Governments, he claims, are "really" motivated by "self-interest"; things such as altruism and self-sacrifice, which are quite appropriate to personal life, have no place in politics. However, Kennan is obviously doing more than simply describing what makes governments tick. As one who has been deeply involved in *making,* and not just observing foreign policy, he seeks to recommend how governments *ought* to conduct their foreign relations. That is, he seeks to discriminate between "good" and "bad," "right" and "wrong" patterns of international behavior, a task that begins to look like moral reflection.

In fact, as the words I quoted make clear, Kennan is "moralizing" all over the place, but in a way that is hardly edifying. Kennan tells us that he does not believe that "the purposes of states are fit subjects for measurement in moral terms"; then, he tells us that the first *duty* of a nation is to itself. (What kind of "duty" is that, and *why* is a nation's first duty to serve itself? In short, to interject "duty" is already to raise moral questions.) He tells us that the "national interest" is all we are capable of knowing; then, he informs us that the pursuit of national interest "can never fail to be con-

21 See, e.g., the interesting essay by R. C. Good, "National Interest and Moral Theory: The 'Debate' Among Contemporary Realists," in *Foreign Policy in the Sixties,* ed. Roger Hilsman and Robert C. Good (Baltimore, 1966), pp. 275, 286.

ducive" to the interests of everyone. (One is tempted to ask how one *knows* that, and particularly so since each nation is supposedly only capable of knowing its own interest.) Nor is Kennan content with this. He recommends that we seek only "decent" national purposes, "unsullied by arrogance" or "delusions of superiority." In other words, national interest is neither self-evident nor self-authenticating; *it must be evaluated*. According to what standards? What are the criteria of "decency"? Finally, it is interesting that after emphasizing the difference in kind that exists between national and personal life, Kennan quite readily ascribes to nations adjectives like "arrogant" and "modest" — terms normally reserved to describe the moral character of individuals.

In short, Kennan is an incurable moralist, but, if I may say so, he is a very exasperating one as well. His arguments raise, but in no way solve, many difficult and perplexing *moral* problems. Indeed, one is tempted to suggest the following proposition: Were it not for the firm grip that the tradition of liberal disillusionment continues to exercise upon American intellectuals, people would long since have agreed that the emperor has no clothes — at least with regard to morality in international affairs. Above all what is so frustrating about Kennan's position is that it makes all sorts of "unconscious" and "unconfessed" moral claims and judgments, while at the same time castigating others for making moral claims and judgments. He continues to moralize without taking the responsibility for doing the job carefully. If you like, he moralizes without a license.

Kennan, like his predecessors, makes a self-contradictory and thoroughly confused assumption: Since governments in their international relations function in what is believed to be an extra-moral arena, the maximum amount of moral benefit for all nations will be produced by refusing to talk about morals. The trouble with this is that it shuts off discussion of the adequacy or inadequacy of particular moral recommendations — whether Wilson's or Metternich's or de Gaulle's or Kennan's — and naively pretends that moral problems in international affairs can be solved by proclaiming all moral recommendations to be a big ruse. Furthermore, Kennan's position is troublesome because in presupposing that all ideals (except his) are a "cover," it assumes that there exists behind the ideals, or underneath them or somewhere, a big, hidden explanation of why a government really behaves as it does.[22] As we shall try to show shortly, both these difficulties seriously retard discussion about foreign policy.

It is sometimes suggested that a more self-conscious moralist like Reinhold Niebuhr, who obviously holds much in common with Kennan, has made significant improvements upon Kennan's view. Frankly, I doubt that Niebuhr carries us in the right direction at all, at least with respect to attempts at revising Kennan. It is true of course that Niebuhr explicitly rejects what he regards as Kennan's undue emphasis upon national "egoism" as a solution to international tensions.[23]

[Kennan's] approach to the problem of national morality is obviously defective. . . . The defect arises from the fact

[22] Just *why* we should treat social behavior in such a monolithic way as to assume that "political man" is primarily motivated by "raw power" has never seemed to me to be demonstrated, but rather assumed, in the writings of Morgenthau and Kennan.

[23] Ed. H. R. Davis and R. C. Good, *Reinhold Niebuhr on Politics* (New York, 1960), pp. 331ff.

that any kind of prudence which estimates common problems from the perspective of a particular interest will define the interest too narrowly. It is necessary, therefore, to draw upon another moral and spiritual resource to widen the concept of interest. The citizens of a nation must have loyalties and responsibilities to a wider system of values than that of the national interest — to a civilization for instance, to a system of justice and to a community of free nations.[24]

But, if we have been correct in our appraisal, the problem with Kennan is not that he has *excluded* moral considerations from his discussion of national interest, and, therefore, is in danger of defining national interest too narrowly. Kennan's most serious problem is that he has made all sorts of moral assumptions about the national interest but will not let anyone else in on *why* he has made these assumptions or what their full implications are for international relations.

Because Niebuhr misunderstands the problem in Kennan, he misunderstands the kind of solution that is required. If there are already moral considerations at work in Kennan's thought about foreign policy — as there most certainly are — then it will not help to be told that we must "add" moral notions to Kennan's conclusions. Rather, we must examine and evaluate the moral assumptions that are already there. Are we willing to accept the implied moral principle that one finds in Kennan (as well as in people like Senator Fulbright), that the interests of all nations will be maximally satisfied insofar as each nation pays primary attention to its own ("decent") interest? Certainly we would not want to accept

[24] *Ibid.,* p. 334.

19

this principle without knowing more about it, although we can, I believe, begin to raise a number of pointed questions.

In any case, Niebuhr's own solution badly muddles the discussion because he uncritically takes over Kennan's explicit, but misleading, language about the disjunction between national interest and morals. It seems to me that Niebuhr at times gets himself into hopeless tangles on this matter. For example, he writes:

> Our power is too great to conform to absolute *or even to relative standards of justice.* . . . We may claim that we use our power in the interest of the total community *with as much justice as is possible for nations,* when all nations are instinctively prompted to consider their own interest, and the interests of others only as they are compatible with their own. But our moral claims ought not go beyond this limit.[25]

Is it or is it not possible for nations to act justly? Niebuhr says first that the U.S. is so powerful it cannot act according to either absolute or relative standards of justice (what other standards are there?); then he says the U.S. can act "with as much justice as is possible for nations," which would seem to be some kind of relative justice, although this is nowhere made clear.

It is significant, I believe, that although Charles Beard and Reinhold Niebuhr were both deeply influenced in the '30's by a "realistic" concern for national interest as a crucial guideline for policy-making, they came to diametrically opposed positions on whether the interest of the United States dictated entry into World War II. Beard remained an unre-

[25] *Nations and Empires* (London, 1959), p. 29; italics added.

constructed isolationist, and Niebuhr became a powerful advocate of military resistance to Hitler. The lesson to be learned from this is one that should have been plain all along: that preoccupation with national interest is a slippery business and can lead in a number of different directions. Undefined and unexamined, the national interest is a very unreliable guide.

Benn and Peters are surely right when they argue that "national interest . . . is an ambiguous concept. In its broad sense the term is significant rather by what it denies than by what it asserts. A state is seeking 'national interest' when it is not concerned with the interests of any groups outside its own jurisdiction, except to the extent that they may affect domestic interests."[26] As they go on to show, this leaves a number of questions unanswered, such as *which* domestic interests are to be served.[27]

But still more important, national interest is often elaborated in political discourse on the basis of specific, although perhaps covert, moral determinations. As Arnold Wolfers has put it:

In every case the interpretation of what constitutes a vital national interest and how much value should be attached to it *is a moral question*. It cannot be answered by reference to alleged amoral necessities inherent in international politics; *it rests on value judgments.* [28]

Wolfers is prepared to concede that there is probably some-

26 S. I. Benn and R. S. Peters, *Principles of Political Thought* (New York, 1964), p. 426.

27 Anyone who doubts the ambiguity of this concept would be well advised to peruse the pages of *The Public Interest,* ed. C. J. Friedrich (New York, 1967).

28 Arnold Wolfers, *Collaboration and Discord* (Baltimore, 1962),

21

thing general and irreducible that is characteristic of national interest — for example, national self-preservation. Yet he contends that most foreign policy problems fall well short of raw survival and involve subtler questions like the protection of treaty rights and the preservation of outlying bases. It is not always easy to deduce decisions regarding such matters directly from the imperative of national survival. On the contrary, in this more complicated area of day-to-day policy making,

> it is a baffling task, almost exceeding human capacity, to compare the value of an increment of national security with the value of human lives, or the value of a continued period of peace with the risks of a more destructive war in the future.[29]

p. 60; italics added. Seabury, *op. cit.,* p. 384, makes this point very nicely in relation to "realists" like Kennan and Morgenthau: There is "an internal contradiction in [the] realist doctrine. To realists, utopianism was errant in that it ignored both power and interests or, at worst, employed idealism to attain impossible goals. But in denigrating the American utopian tradition in world politics, this view also deprecated the moral authority and ethical influence which this tradition had long held. *Such authority and influence could be viewed as a quite special, often indispensable, element of national power. . . .* An assault upon the Wilsonian tradition was, ironically, an assault upon one element of American liberal principles which had immeasurably added weight to United States influence in the world, at least since W. W. I." Italics added.

In his generally cogent and impressive volume, *Discipline of Power* (Boston, 1968), Ambassador George Ball describes the "ultimate purpose of the United States" as the attempt "to build peace not only by protecting our own interests *but by recognizing the interests and the power of other peoples"* (p. 301); italics added. Ball understands that the idea of national interest is properly understood in an international or collective context.

[29] Wolfers, *op. cit.,* p. 62.

In the interests of overall clarity it may be well to keep talk about value judgments and moral judgments separate, as Wolfers does not. It is quite possible, for example, to assign high value to the economic interests of the United Fruit Company in Cuba or the Dominican Republic without necessarily making that value judgment at the same time a moral judgment. For that matter it is possible to define the self-interest of a nation in such a way as to give it supreme value without entailing that the judgment be moral. The statement, "My country, right or wrong" is, I should think, just such an example.

I am inclined, rather, to agree with certain contemporary moral philosophers like Kurt Baier, who argues that the word "moral" *means* "a point of view which furnishes a court of arbitration for conflicts of interest. Hence [to look at a thing morally] cannot be identical with the interest of any particular person or group of persons."[30] And perhaps we should add to this something like G. J. Warnock's recent formulation that whatever else it connotes, the word "moral" means to look

[30] *Moral Point of View* (New York, 1966), p. 96. On Baier's definition, Kennan's following statement would make no sense at all: "Let us, by all means, conduct ourselves at all times in such a way as to satisfy our own ideas of morality. But let us do this as a matter of obligation to ourselves, and not as a matter of obligation to others." *Realities of American Foreign Policy,* p. 47. It is not simply, as John Bennett says, that it is part of our ideas of morality to be obligated to others. *Foreign Policy in Christian Perspective* (New York, 1966), p. 62. On Baier's analysis, to recommend that someone act in disregard of anyone's interests but his own is *not* to make a moral recommendation. Baier's interpretation seems to me perfectly in accord with normal usage.

23

at things such as personal or national interest from the point of view of "the welfare of human beings."[31]

However, this point need not detain us here because, as we have seen, people like Kennan are clearly implying a "moral point of view" in their writings by relating a concern for national interest with the creation of "a better world" for everyone. In fact, it is this covert moralism which underlies, I argue, the tradition of liberal disillusionment. In short, we need to make serious revisions in Kennan's line of argument and, by implication, in that of Reinhold Niebuhr as well. To Kennan, national interest is *not* something to which we do or do not add moral deliberation; it is *related to moral consideration (albeit not very rigorous consideration) from the beginning.*

As Robert Osgood shows in his book, *Ideals and Self-Interest in America's Foreign Relations,*[32] there is no consistently strong tradition in American history in favor of naked national self-interest as the exclusive and all-governing principle of foreign policy. That is not really surprising, given the nature of the American moral creed. For the nature of that creed is clearly universalistic: *"all men* are created equal, and . . . are endowed by their creator with certain unalienable

[31] *Contemporary Moral Philosophy* (London, 1967), p. 67. Warnock goes on: "It is no doubt true that moral doctrines are often used, simply as instruments of repression or aggression, deliberately to do harm rather than good; but even so, it seems that, if it is to be ever pretended that what is enforced is moral doctrine and that it is enforced for that reason, then it must also be at least pretended that some good is likely to be done thereby, or some harm prevented" (p. 58).

[32] Osgood, *op. cit.*

24

rights. . . ." That is, the benefit of all men is increased to the degree that all men obtain freedom of consent and equality of opportunity or participation in political and economic affairs. There is no reason to believe that George Kennan, or the tradition of liberal disillusionment he has perpetuated, does not also hold such moral convictions.[33] The conflict with

[33] Kennan's fondness for the words of John Quincy Adams (see fn. 34) makes this point clear; and it is an extremely important point in understanding Kennan: " 'Wherever the standard of freedom and independence has been or shall be unfurled, there,' Adams said, will be America's heart, her benedictions, and her prayers. 'But she does not go abroad,' he went on, 'in search of monsters to destroy. She is the well-wisher to the freedom and independence of all. She is the champion and vindicator only of her own. . . . She well knows that by once enlisting under other banners than her own, were they even the banners of foreign independence, she would involve herself beyond the power of extrication, in all wars of interest and intrigue . . . which assume the colors and usurp the standards of freedom. The fundamental maxims of her policy would insensibly change from liberty to force. . . .' " *Vietnam Hearings,* p. 115. After two world wars and the Korean War there is a certain quaintness to these words, but Kennan's meaning by using them is plain: the very values America holds dear will necessarily be tarnished when "she goes abroad" and intervenes. Foreign involvement prevents the realization of U.S. values at home and abroad—they change "liberty to force." Cf. *Vietnam Hearings,* p. 118.

In short, there is a fundamental contradiction between democratic values and political (especially military) power. "A democracy is peace-loving. It does not like to go to war. It is slow to rise to provocation. When it has once been provoked to the point where it must grasp the sword, it does not easily forgive its adversary for having produced this situation. . . . Democracy fights in anger—it fights for the very reason it was forced to go to war. . . . Such a war *must be* carried to the bitter end. . . . Our cause is holy; the cost is no consideration; violence must know no limitations short of unconditional surrender." Kennan, *American Diplomacy,* p. 59; italics supplied. To

25

more messianic forms of American idealism is not over the goodness of these values. *It is over their most appropriate means of implementation.* According to Kennan, the way to implement these values most effectively is not by "enlisting under other banners than our own," and by "involving ourselves beyond the power of extrication" — to use Kennan's favorite words from John Quincy Adams. Rather it is by being "champion and vindicator only of our own [nation]."[34]

Similarly, in the debates that rage over foreign policy these days — in intellectual circles at any rate — there is an amazingly broad consensus on the high-level values of the American creed. The point of real conflict comes over policy and implementation. The Administration contends that the chances for realizing the values of the American creed in South Vietnam and in Southeast Asia are made greater by its present policy there. The critics argue exactly the opposite: Present policy makes *less, rather than more, possible* the maximization of value in South Vietnam, Southeast Asia and, for that matter, in the United States as well. It is surely *this* appeal, rather than some neo-isolationistic argument or some claim that "Asia is a loser," that fires the passions of great numbers of liberal intellectuals and students. In short, current controversy over foreign policy is, to an important extent, moral controversy, that is, controversy about what the United States ought to do in order to serve its fundamental values.

Kennan, democratic values must necessarily produce "holy wars" and thus undo themselves. Force can in no way be seen to *serve* democratic values. There is no real possibility of limited war for limited objectives. Just because of his view of American democratic values, then, Kennan resists international military entanglements.

[34] *American Diplomacy,* p. 115.

This fact, of rather remarkable common moral allegiance at a high level, often gets distorted by participants on all sides of the current debates. On the one hand, Administration supporters frequently try to show that the government's detractors are really neo-isolationists who don't care about the rest of the world and seek only to serve themselves. These critics, they allege, do not really believe that *"all* men are created equal" or that *all* men have "certain inalienable rights" and that it is the duty of Americans to promote these rights wherever and however possible. On the other hand, we have the critics' contention that Johnson couldn't possibly be concerned with the legitimate aspirations for freedom of downtrodden people, such as the Vietnamese or the Southeast Asians. No matter what the President or Dean Rusk *say,* they must be (as Niebuhr claims) driven by lust for power, etc., etc.

It is my contention that in this matter *both* sides of the debate are seriously misguided, and that unless things get straightened out, we can expect very little constructive, thoughtful direction on the subject of foreign policy to come out of our experience in Vietnam. I believe that the way each side attempts to discredit the other is rooted in the tradition of liberal disillusionment. And the sooner we move beyond the éxcesses and confusions of that tradition, the better off we shall be. Each side endeavors to prove that the policy recommendations of the other *must* mask a hidden form of self-seeking — isolationism for the critics and megalomania for the Administration. In neither case do I consider the allegations to be true.

On the contrary, the problems at issue in Vietnam are a much subtler, more complicated, congeries of moral and stra-

27

tegic considerations about which there is only one certainty: that men who share common liberal values will differ in evaluating U.S. policy in that country. But we shall not understand the reasons for the differences of opinion and interpretation about U.S. policy in Vietnam by rooting around after "big explanations" and by assuming that the justifications the Administration offers for its position conceal nefarious objectives.

II. THE EXAMPLE OF VIETNAM

I apologize for subjecting the reader to yet another discussion of some aspects of the debate over Vietnam. Nevertheless, I must do this for three reasons: (1) It would be odd indeed for someone to discuss current or recent foreign policy without referring to Vietnam; (2) the case I have been building to this point depends on being able to show that whether finally right or wrong, the justifications proposed by the Administration are not "absurd," or a "snow job" or a "fairy tale" or the product of unmitigated arrogance, whether unconscious or simply unconfessed, and that these justifications mean more or less what they say; (3) the broader foreign policy problems being forced upon us must be viewed, to some degree at least, in the light of Vietnam.

What troubles one most about the endless stream of books, articles and speeches that are so bitterly critical of the Administration — whether Fulbright's *Arrogance of Power,* Draper's *Abuse of Power,* Kahin and Lewis' *U.S. in Vietnam,* or Senator McGovern's famous address, "The Lessons of Vietnam" — is the persistent refusal of the authors even to acknowledge, let alone deal with at length, the arguments of apparently thoughtful, respectable and well-informed people who find plausible some aspects of the Administration's case.

Allow me to cite a few examples from Draper's book, since it is alleged to be "documented and responsible" (Reinhold Niebuhr) as well as "thoughtful, intelligent, and truthful" (Richard Goodwin).

Draper himself admits that Douglas Pike, author of the highly regarded *Viet Cong,*[35] is "a qualified American student" on the subject of the N.L.F.[36] However, Draper *never* mentions

[35] *Viet Cong: The Organization and Techniques of the National Liberation Front of South Vietnam* (Cambridge, Mass., 1966).

[36] Draper, *op. cit.,* p. 129. While Draper seems ready enough to accept Pike's work as authoritative (though, to put it charitably, he has not read the work carefully), other critics are more dubious about *Viet Cong.* The book is bound to cause the critics trouble because it is so richly documented and carefully written and, what is more, it has been called "admirable" by such relatively impartial observers as the late Bernard Fall. Richard Falk's attempts to dismiss the work by casting aspersions on the M.I.T. Center where the book was written, as well as by taking issue with a statement Pike makes in his Preface (see Falk, *op. cit.,* pp. 479-81) are not serious criticisms, for they in no way deal with the substance of Pike's arguments. As to Pike's conclusion about the origins of the N.L.F., Falk in no way refutes the impressive evidence marshalled by Pike—and corroborated, for example, by Fall in *Viet-Nam Witness* (New York, 1966), p. 131—that the insurgency in the South was closely coordinated with the goals of the North Vietnamese.

In a debate with Prof. Noam Chomsky of M.I.T. (an intellectual leader of Resistance), I expected Chomsky to reject Pike outright, which he did not do. Rather, he accepted Pike as authoritative in documentation but wrong in conclusions. It is not, of course, out of the question that an author's conclusions do not follow from his data. But while I have heard this charge from other critics (and have requested detailed evidence), I have yet to be persuaded by Chomsky or anyone else. I find that in general Pike's conclusions flow reasonably from his evidence. It is impossible for the non-expert ever to be sure in matters of such complexity and subtlety, and it is necessary to remain open to new evidence and new argumentation. But, from my

Pike's exhaustive analysis when it is most relevant to the discussion of the "indigenous" character of the Viet Cong or the development of the N.L.F. Pike's analysis simply contradicts Draper's interpretation at several key points.[37] This point of view, the critics have not succeeded in refuting Pike's case with anything like the persuasiveness they have reckoned.

[37] 1. Draper simply asserts, without a shred of supporting evidence, that "it is fair [*sic*] to conclude that until about 1960 the Viet Cong was strictly a Southern enterprise, and until 1965 the Northern contribution was mainly limited to training" (p. 95). Cf. Pike: "Whether led or driven, the D.R.V. clearly did involve itself in the South in terms of doctrinal know-how and civilian cadres and, later, in more material ways. What the D.R.V. cadres brought in particular was organizational ability, and through their efforts the insurgency, previously sporadic and patternless, began to take shape. Insurgency efforts in the 1958-60 period involved violence such as assassination, but few actual armed attacks. . . . *By 1959 an overall directional hand was apparent. The struggle became an imported thing"* (p. 79; cf. p. 80, pp. 322ff.). "The N.L.F. was not simply another indigenous covert group, or even a coalition of such groups. It was an organizational steamroller, nationally conceived and nationally organized, endowed with ample cadres and funds, crashing out of the jungle to flatten the G.V.N. It was not an ordinary secret society. . . . It projected a social construction program of such scope and ambition that of necessity it must have been created in Hanoi and imported. A revolutionary organization must build; it begins with people suffering genuine grievances, who are slowly organized and whose militancy gradually increases. . . . Exactly the reverse was the case with the N.L.F. It sprang full-blown into existence and then fleshed out. The grievances were developed or manufactured almost as a necessary afterthought." *Ibid.,* p. 76.

2. Draper criticizes those who place hope in military security in South Vietnam. "If 'security' were all that mattered, former President Ngo Dinh Diem might have achieved a 'political success' because he had tight control of the country for quite a few years" (p. 164). By contrast, Pike points out, "At one point in time, in 1954, Diem controlled little more than a dozen square blocks of downtown Saigon.

31

does not seem to me a responsible use of sources. Moreover, Draper concludes that P. J. Honey, the British Southeast Asian expert, has studied Vietnam in relation to China "more carefully, perhaps, than anyone else."[38] It is strange, however, that Draper cites Honey only in this connection and never refers to the reasons Honey gives for his rather vigorous sup-

. . . He devoted the 1954-60 period to trying to extend his governmental presence farther into the countryside, and . . . by the time open armed attacks began in 1960 *he had only slight political control over most of the country and still no control at all over certain isolated areas"* (p. 80; italics supplied). He did not control, for example, six N.L.F. bases located in various parts of South Vietnam: e.g., Do Xa in Quang Nai province; Duong Minh Chau in northern Tay Minh province along the Cambodian border, etc. Cf. fn. 10, p. 10. While I would naturally not suggest that "political success" rests exclusively on military security, it appears that this is a much more subtle question than Draper understands. His bald assertions are of little help.

3. Draper contends that Rusk "had to engage in one of his most tortuous intellectual exercises" to argue that since 1960 Hanoi had demanded the acceptance of the N.L.F. "as the sole bargaining representative of the South Vietnamese people" (p. 181). Actually, according to Draper, the 1960 N.L.F. program was an "essentially moderate political mosaic" (p. 181), and "it cannot be argued that it was an outright bid for sole Communist control" (fn., pp. 181-82). Draper cites Pike as evidence in the footnote cited just above! Pike states quite plainly in the pages referred to by Draper: "Early [pre-1962] N.L.F. statements on the subject of coalition implied that the N.L.F. *must dominate any coalition government since it represented all the 'people's elements,'* in fact everyone except the Diemists." Pike, p. 361; "Coalition government with a strong N.L.F. could not be sold within South Vietnam, although it was a useful product for the N.L.F. to market abroad." Pike, p. 362. The whole tone of the relevant chapters in Pike's book, 17-19, is precisely the opposite from what Draper argues! One wonders just *who* is engaging in "tortuous intellectual exercises."

[38] Draper, *op. cit.,* p. 128.

32

port of overall U.S. policy.[39] In addition, Draper deals very critically with the State Department's legal arguments, yet he never once cites either the lengthy and exceedingly careful brief by Professors McDougal, Underwood and Moore which justifies the U.S. position,[40] or the lively and important legal

[39] See P. J. Honey, "The Origins of the Vietnam War," in *Vietnam Seen from East and West,* ed. Sibnarayan Ray (New York, 1966), pp. 21ff.

[40] Under the heading, "The Illegitimate War" (pp. 155-61), Draper provides an exceedingly brief and hasty discussion of the legal questions involved. Strangely, he only deals with the SEATO treaty, and he cites as an "eminent authority" only Prof. W. McMahon Ball (p. 157). Surely thoughtful people would agree that, above all, in the Vietnam debate we need to get the arguments from all sides out on the table where we can deal carefully with them. Draper's failure to examine and respond to the lengthy (260 pp.) Moore, Underwood, McDougal Brief, "The Lawfulness of United States Assistance to the Republic of Viet Nam" (May, 1966) is little short of incredible. (We also have now a more readable but equally extensive defense of the legality of the war by Roger H. Hull and John C. Novogrod, *Law and Vietnam* (New York, 1968). See Falk, *Vietnam War and International Law,* for a compilation of a wide range of views on the legality of U.S. policy. (We propose our own arguments on some of these legal matters in Appendix A, "The Problem of Aggression in the Vietnam War," and Appendix B, "The Problem of Justification for Direct U.S. Military Involvement in Vietnam.")

Though I cannot claim to have acquaintance with all legal discussions of Vietnam, my strong impression is that the defenders of the legality of U.S. policy in Vietnam have done a much more conscientious job of laying out their arguments than have the critics, although the latter have obviously been more vocal. To compare, for example, the McDougal Brief with the analysis of the Lawyers Committee on American Policy Towards Vietnam (which appeared in the *New York Times* of January 15, 1967) is rather appalling. The latter statement is frustratingly brief and (so it seems to this layman) extremely hasty. What is so unfortunate is that Draper hands on the impression that

33

exchanges *on both sides* that have been taking place, for example, in various law journals.[41]

Draper makes a brief, though totally inadequate, reference to the pacification strategy of the U.S. government. But he does not mention *at all* Robert Thompson, whose views on counterinsurgency warfare and pacification are widely respected and who has been an important advisor to the U.S. government in Vietnam. Of course the kind of support Sir Robert gives to President Johnson's policies would be a serious embarrassment to Draper's viewpoint.[42] Finally, it is

the only responsible opinion resides with the critics—see, e.g., Michael Novak, "Stumbling into War and Stumbling Out," in *Vietnam: Crisis of Conscience,* by Robert M. Brown, Abraham J. Heschel and Michael Novak (New York, 1967), p. 27. Novak relies almost completely upon Draper's writings for his arguments. Novak's discussion of the legal matters is no more adequate than Draper's. Cf. Brown's comments in the same volume.

[41] Richard Falk, "International Law and the U.S. Role in the Viet-Nam War," *Yale Law Journal* (1966), p. 75, and "International Law and the U.S. Role in Viet Nam: A Response to Prof. Moore, *YLJ* (1967), p. 76. See also Neill H. Alford, Jr., "Legality of American Military Involvement in Viet Nam: A Broader Perspective," *Yale Law Review* (1966), p. 75; reprinted in Falk, *Vietnam War and International Law*.

[42] Draper's failure to treat Sir Robert Thompson's *Defeating Communist Insurgency: Experiences from Malaya and Vietnam* (New York, 1966) is really inexcusable. As John T. McAlister (author of *Viet Nam: The Origin of the Revolution*) puts it in the *Yale Alumni Magazine* (October, 1967), "Sir Robert . . . has written a carefully structured analysis of the interaction of politics and warfare between 1959 and 1965, but so sound is his insight into the nature of revolutionary war that his book becomes a classic which transcends the particular case of Vietnam, adding a much broader perspective on events taking place there" (p. 15). In my untutored judgment as well, Thompson's is one of the best books on the whole Vietnam problem.

34

perhaps unfair to ask Draper to have familiarized himself with a volume published about the time of his own. But his whole argument would have profitted greatly had he taken the trouble to read the manuscript of Roger Hilsman's study of Vietnam policy in *To Move a Nation*.[43] In short, Draper's book is badly lopsided. At points he makes some telling contributions to the discussion, but great stretches of his book are written with the now familiar implication that only a handful of defensive and befuddled members of the Administration could in any way be sympathetic to U.S. policy. This is both unfair and untrue.

With what I hope is somewhat more objectivity than most of the critics manifest, let us see what can be done to make at least plausible the general justifications that the Administration has provided for its policy. Our objective is to bring into focus the actual range of choices with which the Administration has been faced in its deliberations. We shall divide our discussion into three sections: (A) the expectations created by U.S. involvement in Vietnam; (B) the question as to whether these expectations have been threatened; (C) the problem of whether and to what degree these expectations can be realized.

A. *Expectations and Vietnam*

The years from 1945 to 1953 were critical ones so far as

This sort of oversight is, unfortunately, typical of much of the critical literature; see, e.g, Howard Zinn, *Vietnam: The Logic of Withdrawal* (Boston, 1967).

[43] (New York, 1967). See especially Part IX on Vietnam, although, as we shall indicate below, Parts IV, VII and VIII on Laos, China, Indonesia and Malaysia respectively are also highly relevant. We shall deal more extensively with Hilsman's account below.

United States foreign policy in Asia was concerned. It was a period in which the Truman Doctrine, by means of a series of specific and dramatic policies, encouraged a definite pattern of expectations in Asia. This doctrine, enunciated in March 1947, still retains a good deal of power:

> I believe we must assist free peoples to work out their destinies in their own way. . . . The seeds of totalitarian regimes are nurtured by misery and want. . . . They reach their full growth where the hope of a people for a better life has died. *We must keep that hope alive*.[44]

[44] Quoted in Loewenheim, *op. cit.,* pp. 50-51; italics supplied. In its origins, as H. Bradford Westerfield points out in *Instruments of American Foreign Policy* (New York, 1963), pp. 102-103, the Truman doctrine "relied heavily on the vast material wealth of the U.S., which could be used for economic aid abroad. The military aspects of the struggle were soft pedaled," at least until the outbreak of the Korean War. Thus, as Kennan had formulated the "containment policy," it was *not* primarily a military policy.

At the hands of revisionist historians—e.g., David Horowitz, *The Free World Colossus* (New York, 1965)—the Truman doctrine and, indeed, the whole postwar foreign policy of the U.S., has been charged with stimulating the cold war. And so, in line with the reverse absolutism of much of the New Left, the United States is simply substituted for Russia as the source of all evil. While I am in no position to make a final judgment on this question, I find the arguments of people like Edmund Stillman—himself no great lover of American foreign policy—unexceptionable in these questions: "Anyone who argues in favor of an essentially aggressive U.S. policy in the years 1945-7 must come to terms with the fact that the United States precipitately demobilized at the war's end: American military strength fell from 15 million in 1945 to 1,550,000 in the beginning of 1947, and Congress had instructed the armed forces to cut back to a level below 1 million by the year's end. This is a posture that ill accords with an aggressive, anti-Soviet diplomacy, especially given the scarcity of nuclear weapons in the U.S. arsenal at the time. . . . Further, American forces in 1945,

It would be hard to show that Truman was "just talking" or that he was deviously masking a lust for dominance by means of these high-sounding moralisms. Under Truman's Administration a policy of democratic reform and eventual independence for vanquished Japan was inaugurated, a policy that bore and has continued to bear rather impressive success.[45] On July 4, 1946, Truman presided over the emancipation of the Philippines under a reasonably hopeful democratic government.

In 1950, he reversed a policy of limited disengagement from Asia and responded to the direct military provocation of North Korea against the South. Truman made the decision to fight the Korean War despite several disabilities, it ought to be remembered: The U.S. had already publicly divested itself of all commitments to South Korea; it was faced in the South with an extremely demoralized people and fighting

in accordance with the decisions of the Teheran and Yalta conferences, withdrew from western Czechoslovakia and their advanced positions in Germany to agreed zonal boundaries at a time when it was already evident that, particularly in Poland and Rumania, the USSR was embarked on a cynical program aimed at incorporating the region, not merely into a Soviet security zone, but into a Soviet imperial system." Herman Kahn, *et al, Can We Win in Vietnam?* (New York, 1968), fn. 6, p. 147. Cf. Zbigniew K. Brzezinski, *Soviet Bloc* (New York, 1960), esp. pp. 51ff. It is gratifying to find even such critical authors as Falk conceding that the Truman doctrine "at that time, was closely and sensibly related to certain geopolitical realities. . . . Global communism was a reality to be resisted and feared. . . ." *Vietnam War and International Law,* p. 505.

45 See, e.g., Edwin O. Reischauer, *United States and Japan* (New York, 1965), esp. chaps. 1, 10-14. See also his *Beyond Vietnam: The United States and Asia* (New York, 1967). Cf. "Our Dialogue with Japan," *Foreign Affairs* (January, 1967).

force; along with South Korea, the U.S. bore 90% of the military costs, and it was fighting on behalf of the incredibly autocratic, repressive and corrupt administration of Syngman Rhee. Nevertheless, in defense of his doctrine, Truman decided it was worthwhile to "keep that hope alive" in South Korea.[46] As Dexter Perkins has written in *The Diplomacy of a New Age:*

> The defense [for the Korean War] on which the Truman Administration rested was . . . that submission to aggression in Korea would inevitably lead to new challenges to the existing international order. This, of course, cannot be proved. But the hypothesis was not unreasonable. And *it underlines the strong bent of American foreign policy to stress broad moral considerations rather than specific and special interests.*[47]

Despite the ambiguities and uncertainties intrinsic to the direction of the Truman Doctrine in Asia, the United States was very concretely developing hopes and expectations in favor of assisting "free peoples to work out their destinies in their own way." By its actions it had created what we might call "regional momentum," in which a prosperous, democratic Japan began to be the model of development, rather than Communist China.[48]

Against the background of the Truman Doctrine, which

[46] For an exceptionally good account of Truman's role in the Korean War see John W. Spanier, *Truman-MacArthur Controversy and the Korean War* (New York, 1965). See also Westerfield, *op. cit.,* chaps. 7 and 8.

[47] Dexter Perkins, *Diplomacy of a New Age* (Bloomington, Ind., 1967), pp. 107-108; italics added.

[48] Reischauer, *Beyond Vietnam,* pp. 118-119.

also advocated support to "free peoples who are resisting attempted subjugation by armed minorities or by outside pressure," the U.S. became involved in South Vietnam in 1954. Fourteen years later it is all very well to say that as a "neo-colonial power" we intervened arbitrarily in an essentially "nationalistic" and "civil" struggle. I have as yet been unable to uncover any prominent observer who interpreted our involvement in Vietnam in those terms in the mid-1950's. In 1956, Hans Morgenthau praised President Diem for "the miracle" he had wrought in South Vietnam.[49] In 1955, though he shrewdly warned against over-reliance on military power,[50] Reinhold Niebuhr wrote of our involvement

[49] *Teach-Ins: U.S.A.*, ed. I. Menashe and Ronald Radosh (New York, 1967), p. 206. Note also on the same page Morgenthau's total error in assessing the status and future of Laos.

While one certainly cannot hold people to opinions they expressed more than ten years ago, it is interesting to note the radical changes in Morgenthau's assessment of U.S. policy in Asia. Today, he argues, "we must learn to accommodate ourselves to the predominance of China on the Asian mainland." *Vietnam and the United States,* pp. 63-64. In 1951, he wrote: "Our real interest is in those people as people. It is because communism is hostile to that interest that we want to stop it. But it happens that the best way of doing both things is to do just exactly what the peoples of Asia want to do and what we want to help them do, which is to develop a soundness of administration of these new governments. . . ." *In Defense of National Interest* (New York, 1951), p. 260; cf. p. 259. I cite this simply to point out the fairly unanimous assumption among most intellectuals in the early 1950's that communism was something worth stopping.

[50] Actually, U.S. policy in Vietnam from 1954 on apparently was *not* characterized by an over-emphasis on military aid. Arthur and Don R. Larson, hardly staunch defenders of our Vietnam policy, write: "Of total aid from 1953 to 1961, less than one-fourth was classified as military, and more than three-fourths economic. Some

in South Vietnam: "We are certainly more disinterested than the French in *desiring only* the health of a new nation, and its sufficient strength *to ward off the Communist* peril from the north."[51] The then Senator John F. Kennedy summarized in 1956 what seems to have been the general American sentiment: He spoke of "the amazing success of President Diem in meeting firmly and with determination the major political and economic crises which had heretofore continually plagued Vietnam."[52] And as late as 1960, Kennedy could reaffirm that the South Vietnamese "began to release and harness the latent power of nationalism to create an independent, anti-Communist Vietnam."[53]

idea of the relatively small size of the military side may be seen from the announcement, on May 5, 1960, that the Military Assistance and Advisory Group would be increased by the end of the year from 327 to 685." "What Is Our Commitment in Viet-Nam?" *Viet-Nam Reader,* ed. M. G. Raskin and B. Fall (New York, 1965), p. 101.

[51] "The Limits of Military Power," reprinted in *World Crisis and American Responsibility,* ed. E. W. Lefever (New York, 1958), p. 120. The essay first appeared in *The New Leader* (May 30, 1955); italics added.

[52] A Senate speech made by Senator J. F. Kennedy in June, 1956, reprinted in *Strategy of Peace,* ed. Allan Nevins (New York, 1960), p. 61.

[53] Kennedy's own comment in 1960. *Ibid.,* p. 61. Cf. fn. 8 by Allan Nevins, p. 62. It is important to note that one of the very few senatorial dissenters in 1954 regarding U.S. involvement in Vietnam was none other than the present "hawk," Senator John Stennis. He admitted in 1954 that a Communist takeover in Southeast Asia would have "serious consequences," but "it would carry far worse consequences for the U.S. and the rest of the free world for us to become involved in a long, costly and indecisive war that left us without victory." Quoted by Don Oberdorfer, "Noninterventionism, 1967 Style," *New York Times Magazine* (September 17, 1967), p. 104. On

When President Eisenhower issued his now famous "conditional" commitments to President Diem[54] no one, to my knowledge, rose up and coolly pointed out that failure to make the prescribed reforms on Diem's part would naturally result in the United States turning South Vietnam loose to fend for itself. The "conditions" set down by Eisenhower (and Kennedy, for that matter) were in the nature of "hortatory" conditions.[55] They were made in the context of the 1950's when there was an almost universal predisposition by Americans to regard Communist subversion and expansion as an extremely serious threat. After all, in 1953 Reinhold Niebuhr

the other hand, Senator Mike Mansfield, in 1953, stated: ". . . The military prospects of the non-Communist forces in Indochina are improving, . . . and that continuing American assistance is justified and essential . . . and that the issue in this war which so many people would like to forget is the continued freedom of the non-Communist world, the containment of Communist aggression and the welfare and security of our own country." *Ibid.,* p. 106.

It ought to be emphasized here that the climate of opinion among "liberals" changed noticeably from the period in April, 1954, when the U.S. was busy trying to stay out of a "colonial war," to the post-1954 period when, most people were convinced, the U.S. was "certainly more disinterested than the French"—in Reinhold Niebuhr's words quoted above. See Chalmers M. Roberts, "The Day We Didn't Go to War," *Viet-Nam Reader,* pp. 57ff.

[54] See Draper, *op. cit.,* pp. 40-41; cf. McDougal Brief, p. 61, for a fuller account of the Eisenhower-Diem exchanges.

[55] My judgment on this is confirmed in Dennis Duncanson's *Government and Revolution in Vietnam* (London, 1968), pp. 277-78. "President Eisenhower had warned Diem from the beginning that American aid must be matched by Vietnamese performance. Unfortunately, the diplomacy of that particular communication stopped short of indicating what would be done in the event of non-performance. . . ."

was describing the "Communist peril" in language that rivaled the expressions of John Foster Dulles. At that time communism, for Niebuhr, was a "noxious demonry."

> If we seek to isolate the various causes of an organized evil which *spreads terror and cruelty throughout the world and confronts us everywhere* with faceless men who are immune to every form of moral and political suasion, we must inevitably begin with the monopoly of power which communism establishes.[56]

The point is that viewed in the tense context of the Stalinist period, our involvement in and development of South Vietnam was simply assumed to be a worthwhile endeavor, although many people, including Senator Kennedy, were urging us to emphasize social and economic transformation as more important in the long run than military preparedness.[57] Nor, as the studies of Hoang Van Chi, P. J. Honey, Robert Shaplen, George K. Tanham, Donald Lancaster and Dennis Duncanson have made clear, was there at that time any reason to equate Vietnamese nationalism with the communism of Ho Chi Minh.[58] The ruthlessness with

[56] Niebuhr, "Why Is Communism So Evil?" in *Christian Realism and Political Problems* (New York, 1953), reprinted in *World Crisis,* p. 50; italics supplied. It is worth noting that even Reischauer, who wrote about Asia more prophetically than most in 1955, referred to communism "as if it were a single great wave threatening to sweep over Asia," as he himself admits. Reischauer, *Beyond Vietnam,* p. 33.

[57] So were others, including Vice-President Hubert Humphrey. See his recollections of his views regarding South Vietnam in the middle-'50's, recorded in the *New York Times* (June 23, 1968).

[58] Hoang Van Chi, *From Colonialism to Communism: A Case History of North Vietnam* (New York, 1965), esp. pp. 20-26, 29ff., 126; Honey, *op. cit.;* Robert Shaplen, "The Leaders: Today and To-

which Ho eliminated all anti-Communist nationalists from his ranks, and the extreme terrorism he employed to solidify the power of his party in North Vietnam between 1954 and

morrow," *Asia* (Winter, 1966) and *The Lost Revolution* (New York, 1966), pp. 254ff.; George K. Tanham, "Nationalism and Revolution," *Asia* (Winter, 1966); Donald Lancaster, *The Emancipation of French Indochina* (London, 1961), esp. fn. 28, p. 371: ". . . to millions of Vietnamese a Communist regime was abhorrent"; Dennis Duncanson, *Government and Revolution in Vietnam,* esp. pp. 140ff. Since Duncanson's work is clearly not just another book on Vietnam but, in the judgment of experts in the field such as Prof. Harry Benda of Yale, is an exceptionally well-informed work of long-range significance, it is necessary to add a word about the volume. Its central theses, while by no means uncritical of U.S. policy, will give no particular comfort to the views presently institutionalized in critical circles. Whether Duncanson's basic themes are correct or not I am not competent to judge. But (much as with Pike's book) they are themes that must be dealt with by the critics. Prof. Paul Mus of Yale has registered some objections to Duncanson's view of Ho Chi Minh in *The New Journal* (May 12, 1968), although he apparently finds much that is acceptable in the book. How one adjudicates between the differing judgments of scholars of deep competence and experience in Vietnam, I do not know. As with all the other complex aspects of this problem, one can only do his best in weighing arguments and evidence. But, once again, this sort of dilemma ought to teach caution and reserve.

There is a fundamental theme running throughout Duncanson's book that seems to me very sound and, in the light of much recent talk about settlements in Vietnam, in need of special emphasis. This theme has to do with the essentially fragmented and "anarchic" political conditions that have characterized Vietnamese history for so long. Contrary to the popular argument that all Vietnamese possess an intense sense of national unity and will therefore never be content with anything short of reunification (e.g., *Newsweek,* [December 16, 1968], p. 46), Duncanson contends: "the conclusion to be drawn from this study of Vietnamese history is that nationalism has been entirely negative and an excuse for sectarian bids for power" (p. 375).

1956, lent a good deal of credibility to Western distaste for Communist methods.[59]

Finally, the United States embarked upon its policy in South Vietnam against the clear and present danger of a Communist guerrilla victory in Malaya. The British and the Malayan nationalists showed an amazing amount of ingenuity in finally defeating the insurgents by 1956 (although it took twelve years!).[60] But the Malayans saw then, and have continued to see, their own security and independence very much wrapped up with the future of Vietnam. Though Malaysia has received no aid from the United States and can, therefore, hardly be considered a "lackey" of the U.S. government, still, as early as 1958, Tunku Abdul Rahman, Prime Minister of Malaysia, declared Malaysia's "solidarity" with South Vietnam in their common struggle against Hanoi's "methods of infiltration and subversion."[61]

[59] It has always seemed to me that the rather grisly record of events in North Vietnam—see Hoang Van Chi, *op. cit.;* Lancaster, *op. cit.;* Honey, *op. cit.;* Gerard Tongas, *L'enfer communiste au nord Viet-Nam* (Paris, 1960)—as well as the world political context of Stalinism, and the Korean War must surely be figured in as justifiable reasons for much of the pro-Diem sentiment that abounded in the United States in the '50's. It is these things, among others, that Robert Scheer leaves out of account altogether in his *How the United States Got Involved in Vietnam* (Fund for the Republic, 1965).

[60] For a brief account, see A. Doak Barnett, *Communist China and Asia,* (New York, 1960), pp. 485-88. It is interesting, in this connection, that President Kennedy cited as one important reason for staying in South Vietnam the necessity of denying to China "an improved geographic position for an assault on Malaya. . . ."

[61] "Malaysia: Key Area in Southeast Asia," *Foreign Affairs* (July, 1965), p. 667. Rahman goes on: "The long history of aggressive action by North Vietnam and its intensifications of hostilities in recent

Thus, the attempt to begin to build a pattern of "regional momentum" in Asia certainly did not seem to be an illicit or mistaken undertaking when it was initiated in the '50's. The expectations the United States was cultivating — that non-Communist political and social developments were worth a try — seemed not only very much in tune with our own values and hopes but remarkably in touch with the aspirations of many Asians themselves.[62] Prime Minister Rahman summarizes these expectations better than anyone else who has treated the subject:

months more than justify the firm stand taken by the U.S. We in Malaysia fully support Washington's actions."

[62] Perhaps this is the point to comment on Oglesby's thesis about economic or commercial interests lying behind and "really" motivating U.S. foreign policy. He contends that in Vietnam—as in every other part of the world—the U.S. defines a country as "free when Americans . . . are free to do business in it. . . ." Oglesby, *op. cit.,* p. 115. But while one might show that in *specific cases* foreign policy is determined by economic opportunities, Oglesby's case is *least persuasive* where it is intended to pay off—in Vietnam! Unlike the case of the fruit companies in Latin America, he is able to adduce nothing at all conclusive, except the assertion that Vietnam is a "key" to wide, long-range possibilities. He also argues (predictably) that the war is good for the U.S. economy.

Undoubtedly, economic concerns are bound up with our interests in Asia—particularly with respect to Japan. To admit this is common sense. What is not proven by Oglesby (but what he must prove to sustain his thesis) is that our economic concern in Japan is our *only* interest in Asia. Quite simply, what one would like to know is *who* is determining policy exclusively on the basis of business interests. President Johnson, as Oglesby implies? He would seem to be paying a big price, politically, to favor these alleged business interests in Vietnam. Actually, Oglesby's thesis—as one all-explanatory thesis—approaches the absurd. Cf. Reischauer's much saner analysis of economic interests in Asia in *Beyond Vietnam,* pp. 53-57.

Why should Asian nations allow themselves to be attracted to the alluring prospects of an economic advancement claimed by the Communists when it means the unnecessary surrender of their liberties? Asian nations can see for themselves the remarkable resurgence of Japan through the spirit of free enterprise and democracy. Even a small country like ours has been able, under the aegis of democracy, to achieve success without the sacrifices which communism demands. By comparison North Vietnam and North Korea expose the myth of supposing that communism is a guaranteed solution to the problems presented by economic security.[63]

If indeed it was a mistake to have gone into Vietnam in the first place it was, nevertheless, a plausible decision backed, at that time, by a wide range of support in this country. But mistake or no, the decision to intervene definitely extended the pattern of expectations which our policy was creating in Asia. And that fact carried with it responsibilities which could not be taken lightly.

B. *The Expectations and the Threat*

The exact character of the threat to the objectives of U.S. foreign policy in Asia has been hotly contested. And well it might be, because determining whether there *is* a threat, and of what it consists, is obviously one of the key considerations in the determination of policy.

We have already heard Draper's view: the notion that a setback for communism in South Vietnam would be decisive

[63] *Op. cit.,* p. 670. See J. A. Kim, "The Long March of North Korea's Kim," *New York Times Magazine* (February 25, 1968), for a discussion of North Korea relevant to Rahman's observations.

for Southeast Asia is a "political fairytale." This judgment does not accord in any way with the views of Roger Hilsman in *To Move a Nation*. Hilsman claims that in 1961, though President Kennedy was not entirely happy about it, he could not refuse to provide added military and economic support to South Vietnam. "Or at least he could not refuse to give more of the same kind of assistance without disrupting . . . *the fabric of the security structure of the region, where so many countries had based their policy on continued American involvement*."[64] For quite definitely Kennedy believed that what was taking place in Vietnam was a very serious threat to the expectations of American policy — the threat of "concealed aggression." In a letter to President Diem in 1961, Kennedy wrote: "The campaign of force and terror now being waged against your people and your government is supported and directed from the outside by the authorities in Hanoi."[65] As early as 1958, writes Hilsman, reflecting Kennedy's view, "a major attack was being launched. It was indirect, but still *it was aggression* — through the guerrilla tactics and techniques of 'internal war.' "[66] Nor, despite statements about its being "their war,"[67] did Kennedy's determination to meet the

[64] Hilsman, *op. cit.,* p. 420; italics added.

[65] See McDougal Brief, p. 32, for the text.

[66] Hilsman, *op. cit.,* p. 419. See Appendix A: The Problem of Aggression in the Vietnam war.

[67] Cited in Hilsman, p. 497. This passage is quoted with almost religious devotion by all the Kennedy exiles. As I read the entire passage in its context, it strikes me that this is another of those "hortatory" utterances to which I called attention above. I do not get the impression President Kennedy meant to imply that if the necessary reforms were not made in the government of South Vietnam, the U.S. would withdraw. And I think this interpretation is all the more un-

threat during his brief administration diminish. Shortly before his death he made a statement which most Kennedy "exiles" find it convenient to overlook:

What helps win the war, we support; what interferes with the war effort, we oppose. . . . This is the text which I think every agency and official of the United States Government must apply to all our activities. . . . We are not there to see a war lost. . . .[68]

Now two questions arise: First, are there reasons for thinking that Kennedy's judgment as to the nature of the threat was right? Second, was it reasonable to gauge this threat in terms of the "security structure of the region"? As to the first question, Douglas Pike's *Viet Cong* makes plausible the main lines of Kennedy's and Johnson's appraisal of the threat,[69] and it places the burden of proof back on the shoulders of critics like Draper. As one who has picked his way very carefully through Pike's painstaking and genuinely well-documented book, I can only rub my eyes in disbelief at the superficial judgments Draper has made on the role

likely when the statement is read together with the next statement we quote. Only ten days separate these two utterances. Kennedy spoke about "their war" on September 2, 1963. He spoke about "winning the war" on September 12, 1963.

[68] *Ibid.,* pp. 505-506. Hilsman admits: "This statement took us a bit farther down the road."

[69] See Appendix A. As I state in the Appendix, I would have serious reservations about using the various State Department White Papers as a basis for this interpretation. Seen in the proper context, they are supplementary. I have in mind *A Threat to Peace, North Viet-Nam's Effort to Conquer South Viet-Nam* (1961), and *Aggression from the North, the Record of North Viet-Nam's Campaign to Conquer South Viet-Nam* (1965).

of North Vietnam in the South. The whole point of Pike's book is that the N.L.F. movement in the South was, even in its origins, clearly tied to an "expansionist drive by the North Vietnamese,"[70] and that the organizational efficacy of the N.L.F. — which is its secret of success — was generated in North Vietnam.[71]

Naturally, this does not mean that Southerners have not comprised the great majority of N.L.F. membership, but it does mean that Kennedy's judgment about the campaign of terror being "supported and directed from the outside," or Hilsman's use of the word "aggression," are not without foundation. Nor, by implication, is Secretary Rusk's use of the word "aggression" since 1961 simply senseless or inconsistent rhetoric, as Draper contends.

Furthermore, as Hilsman, Pike, Thompson, Duncanson and Honey argue, the N.L.F. has never been "representative" of nationalistic sentiment in the South, which became increasingly antagonistic to excesses of the Diem regime. Honey writes:

> It is of interest to note in passing that the Communists failed to persuade a single South Vietnamese of any note or reputation to accept any office in the Front. [And] . . . throughout the whole series of *coups d'état* against . . . Diem and his successors, none of the anti-government movements ever sought to make common cause with the Viet Cong or seek assistance from it.[72]

Whether the similar views of a variety of authorities are finally correct I am not qualified to say. They certainly seem plaus-

[70] Pike, *op. cit.*, p. 53.

[71] *Ibid.*, p. 78.

[72] Honey, *op. cit.*, p. 29. Cf. Duncanson, *op. cit.*, pp. 297-99.

ible. At least they have never been refuted seriously by any of the many critics I have read.

The second question to be answered is this: Even if the North represents a threat to the hopes and aspirations of the great number of non-Communist South Vietnamese — including the Catholics, the Buddhists, the Cao Dai, the Hoa Hoa and the Montagnards — is there anything to Kennedy's and Johnson's view that the threat is to an area broader than simply South Vietnam? Like everything else in the decisions over Vietnam, this is a difficult question to answer with absolute certainty. I find the comments of Australian editor Donald Horne very much to the point:

> One of the ideas of the year was that a successful Hanoi, once it had absorbed South Vietnam (and maybe Laos, and maybe Cambodia) would then settle down into a mild Titoist regime. . . . Another was that an American collapse would not really cause a stampede of fear in the rest of Southeast Asia. One cannot "prove" that any of these comforting ideas is wrong. One can point to possible events that would make them wrong. . . . The real answer is simply another cliché: *it would be a damnfool risk to take*.[73]

One can point to the assertions of support for U.S. policy — some of them very vigorous — from many of South Vietnam's neighbors — Malaysia, Thailand, Laos, the Philippines, Japan, South Korea, Singapore,[74] at times Cambodia,[75] and

[73] Donald Horne, "Reason—and the Murders and Miseries of Asia," *Vietnam Seen from East and West,* p. 183.

[74] A few selected relevant dispatches from the *New York Times* on expressions of support from these various countries are as follows: "Thant Is Disputed by Seven Asian Envoys on His View of War" (January 14, 1967); "Singapore Leader's Vietnam Stand Elicits

even, more recently, Indonesia,[76] not to mention Australia and

Echoes; Other Asian Officials Concur in Support of U.S. Policy" (March 29, 1967); "Non-Red Nations in Asia Take Hope; U.S. Stand in Vietnam and Rift in Peking Encourage Leaders in Southeast" (April 23, 1967); "Sato Praises U.S. on Vietnam Policy" (November 15, 1967); "Laos, Thailand and War; Many Asians Link Security of Region to Continuing U.S. Pressure on Hanoi" (October 20, 1967). See also Thanat Khoman, "Which Road for Southeast Asia?" *Foreign Affairs* (July, 1964), pp. 628ff. And see Robert Shaplen's fascinating account of Premier Lee Kuan Yew of Singapore in *The New Yorker* (December 12, 1967). Cf. Duncanson, *op. cit.,* p. 5.

[75] Particularly in light of the startling about-face of Prince Norodom Sihanouk on the question of Cambodian sanctuaries and U.S. policy, a statement he made in March, 1967 is very important: "Sihanouk of neutralist Cambodia has been quoted as having given thanks for the American presence in Southeast Asia, which he often denounces in public. The outspoken Cambodian chief of state is reported to have told Australian diplomats, among others, that he is well aware of the American counter-pressure to the Communists adhering to Hanoi and Peking." *New York Times* (March 29, 1967). Cf. Duncanson, *op. cit.,* p. 5.

[76] Because of the Indonesian Foreign Minister's earlier antagonism to the U.S. presence in Vietnam (duly recorded in Kahin and Lewis, *op. cit.,* pp. 309-310 and Draper, *op. cit.,* p. 123), Robert Shaplen's reports are of the greatest interest: "The widely held fear that if we stay in Vietnam much longer we will lose whatever worthwhile influence we might continue to have in Southeast Asia in the future does not accord with the views of most of the statesmen and political observers I have talked with in all parts of the region during the last year. They include such socialist leaders as Prime Minister Lee Kuan Yew of Singapore and Foreign Minister Adam Malik of Indonesia, who, eager though they, too, are to see the war ended, firmly believe that the manner of our disengagement is perhaps the most important single question that Asia has been confronted with since 1945. Along with many others who have been critical of our past Vietnam policies, both Malik and Lee feel that a failure to extricate ourselves with dignity and with substantial guarantees would do more than anything else to bring about the bankruptcy of American foreign policy in this

New Zealand. One could quote at length the views of respectable journalists who have argued for some version of a modified domino theory.[77] One could cite the evidence of direct North Vietnamese military activity in Laos (since the '50's) part of the world, and probably in other parts as well." *New Yorker,* (January 20, 1968).

[77] Although Tom Wicker of the *New York Times* has since altered his position on the overall wisdom of the war, his dispatches from Asia in February, 1967, provided support for a modified domino theory. For example, "There is enough truth in the domino theory that it ought to be restated as perhaps the 'open door theory.' That is, if the technique of internal subversion assisted by a neighboring nation were successful in South Vietnam, it would greatly encourage the use of the same technique for attempted conquest elsewhere in the world. Even worse, a victory made possible by some form of American failure to honor its pledge to defend South Vietnam would make such victories elsewhere appear easy" (February 12, 1967). Cf. *Times* (February 9, 1967): "Another factor seems undeniably to be the increasing confidence the leaders of the region have in an American 'umbrella' of protection over Asia, as a result of the Johnson Administration's policy in Vietnam."

Seymour Topping produced two essays for the *New York Times Magazine* in early 1966 that remain close to the best expositions of a modified domino theory I have seen: "Southeast Asia Isn't Scared of the Chinese Dragon" (January 16, 1966), and "Next on Peking's Hit Parade?" (February 20, 1966). (Topping is the *Times'* chief Southeast Asian correspondent.) For example, he writes in the first essay: "The maintenance of a United States military deterrent to Communist aggression will be no less essential to shield Southeast Asia than it has been in the defense of Western Europe."

Or, one might mention Robert Shaplen's essay in *Foreign Affairs* (October, 1967) entitled "Viet Nam: Crisis of Decision." He writes: "In the final analysis, the degree of American determination to support nationalist development in Viet Nam and elsewhere in Southeast Asia, and to back up its support with multifarious resources, will prove the key factor, politically and economically more than militarily" (p. 110).

and its indirect activity in Thailand.[78] One could mention Jean Lacouture's dictum: "Hanoi seeks to rebuild under its own rule or influence, the components of former French Indochina."[79] Of course it must be conceded that the point is not absolutely proved. But surely reasonable men would agree that a policy-maker would be a "damnfool" not to weigh seriously the threat of North Vietnam to the area. Whatever else it may be, the proposition "Whether we like it or not, our Asian interests are tied to a great extent to the outcome of the Vietnam war,"[80] is *not* a fairytale.

[78] See Topping, "Next on Peking's Hit Parade?" for a discussion of North Vietnamese activity in both Laos and Thailand. Selected relevant dispatches from the *New York Times:* "British Say Hanoi Has Units in Laos; Foreign Office Publishes Indian-Canadian [I.C.C.] Report" (August 23, 1966); "Hanoi Refugees Worry Thailand" (May 23, 1967); "Laos, Thailand and War" (October 20, 1967); "Laotians Accuse Forces of Hanoi" (December 27, 1967); "New Red Pressure in Asia Is Feared; U.S. Voices Concern Over Laos, Cambodia, Thailand—Renews Assurances" (December 28, 1967). See also Maynard Parker, "Americans in Thailand," *Atlantic* (December, 1966); and the excellent essay by Peter Braestrup, "The 'Little Vietnam' in Thailand: How the Guerrillas Came to Koh Noi," *New York Times Magazine* (December 10, 1967).

[79] Jean Lacouture, "Uncle Ho Defies Uncle Sam," *New York Times Magazine* (March 28, 1965). See also, Robert A. Scalapino, "We Cannot Accept a Communist Seizure of Vietnam," *New York Times Magazine* (December 11, 1966), and Oscar Gass, "China, Russia and the U.S.," *Commentary* (April, 1967).

[80] Neil Sheehan, reply (October 16, 1966) to a criticism of his moving essay in the *New York Times Magazine* (October 9, 1966), "Not a Dove, but No Longer a Hawk." Having painted a rather bleak picture of the Vietnam situation (one ought to read this article when he finds himself becoming hawkish), Sheehan was accused of not going far enough. His reply should not be overlooked as it is by Zinn,

Furthermore, it does not seem unreasonable that a policy-maker — given the expectations created by the U.S. — would be concerned about the role of China in Asia. Of course it has been a favorite maneuver of the Administration's critics, including, more recently, many of the Kennedy exiles, to claim that the fear of Chinese expansionism is a fabrication of Dean Rusk and a handful of mindless souls who are fifteen years out of date. These critics delight in pointing out that communism is not monolithic and that China's expansionist designs, as well as her capabilities, have been pathologically overrated.[81] At one point James Reston went so far as to suggest that by emphasizing the danger of China to Southeast Asia, Rusk was invoking the image of the "yellow peril." (Reston himself later admitted this was "silly" — though

op. cit., pp. 49-50. Draper does not take it seriously enough; see his book, pp. 101-102.

[81] This is a favorite line of the Kennedy exiles. Cf. Arthur Schlesinger, Jr., "A Middle Way Out of Vietnam," *New York Times Magazine* (September 18, 1966), pp. 114-15, and *The Bitter Heritage: Vietnam and American Democracy, 1941-1966* (Boston, 1967), which is an elaboration of this essay. See also John Kenneth Galbraith, "The Galbraith Plan to End the War," *New York Times Magazine* (November 12, 1967), p. 132.

As to Schlesinger's book, *The Bitter Heritage,* I could not agree more with the review by David Halberstam, *op. cit.:* "The failing of this book is that Schlesinger has not used the same tough standards on President Kennedy as he has on President Johnson. He reads selectively from the Kennedy record. . . . A good historian like Schlesinger should pay more attention to the question of which President really had more freedom of action in Vietnam:, one who took over when there were only 600 Americans there, as advisors, or one who took over when a commitment of 16,000 had failed. . . . Besides, the key Johnson advisors in much of this have been Kennedy men— Taylor, McNamara, Bundy, and indeed Rusk."

if one were striving for accuracy "malicious" might be a better adjective.[82]

The *New York Times* rendered a rare service in pointing out editorially what any careful observer of the Vietnam scene has known for a long time: If anyone gave currency to the notion that China is more than a paper threat in Asia, it was President Kennedy.[83] In his first State of the Union message in January, 1961, Kennedy warned of the "relentless pressures of the Chinese Communists." He elaborated this theme in several press conferences in 1963:

> I would regard that combination of weak countries around [China], seven hundred million [Chinese] people, a Stalinist internal regime, and nuclear powers, and *a government determined on war* as a means of bringing about the ultimate success, as potentially a more dangerous situation than any we faced since the end of the second world

[82] The "yellow peril" notion was manifestly racist and very closely allied with the doctrine of the survival of the fittest. To impute that sort of meaning to the Administration's position is not unusual among some critics. It is not worthy of Mr. Reston, and I should have expected a more profound apology. In reality, as the quotation below makes clear, the only difference between President Kennedy's formulations about China and Mr. Rusk's was the number of Chinese each cited (Kennedy, 800,000,000; Rusk, one billion). According to his campaign literature, Senator Eugene McCarthy also indulged in talk of "yellow peril" after hearing Dean Rusk (October 16, 1967).

[83] See the editorial, "Kennedy vs. Kennedy" (November 28, 1967). I did not find Roger Hilsman's rejoinder (December 5, 1967) persuasive. Hilsman contends, as he does in his book, that by making the struggle in Vietnam "our" war rather than "theirs" the aims of the war had been changed. Hilsman's letter does not begin to make this distinction clear, nor do I think his book does. (See below for an examination of this point.)

war. . . .[84] China is so large, looms so high just beyond the frontiers, that if South Vietnam went, it would not only give them an improved geographic position for an assault on Malaya, but would also give the impression that the wave of the future in Southeast Asia was China and the Communists.[85]

Nor were Kennedy's views, and their reaffirmation in the more recent statements of the Johnson Administration, altogether out of line with the current views of some experts on China. In a very influential book written in 1960, *Communist China and Asia,* Professor A. Doak Barnett wrote:

It is eminently clear that Communist China represents the most dangerous threat to American political and economic, as well as security, interests throughout Asia. If the United States is to achieve its aims in the region — to prevent domination of Asia by any single state, *to support the principles of independence and self-determination in that area, and to encourage the political and economic growth of democratic, non-Communist states* — it must not only evolve adequate security measures to deter Chinese Communist military expansionism; it must also devote primary attention to the need for more positive and effective measures to assist in developing viable, independent, non-Communist states.[86]

[84] Hilsman, *op. cit.,* p. 339; italics added.

[85] Editorial, *op. cit.*

[86] Barnett, *op. cit.,* p. 461; italics added. Though today we would not put things exactly as Barnett did, one wonders where the present critics of our views of China were when these words were written. So far as I can tell, in 1960 Barnett's outlook was widely shared.

In the Senate Hearings on China held in March, 1966, Professor Barnett appears to have modified somewhat his assessment of China's actual military threat in Asia, and he urged that the U.S. view skeptically the extravagant assertions of Lin Piao.[87] Nevertheless, he continued to stress that China is still a source of deep instability in Asia. He was joined in this view by Professor J. K. Fairbank, who was "insistent on maintaining a policy of containment of China, 'an attitude of firmness backed by force,' because 'the Chinese are not more amenable to pure sweetness and light than other revolutionaries.' "[88]

In December, 1967, Barnett joined a group of political scientists and historians in publicly articulating what appears to be a widespread evaluation of the present character of the Chinese threat in Asia. The scholars spoke of the increasing inclination of China to "project her power abroad" by means of "encouraging and abetting" revolutionary movements in several Asian countries.[89] Or, as Professor Edwin O. Reischauer puts it in *Beyond Vietnam,* "China's greatest threat, I feel, has been and will continue to be not a military threat but a more subtle one of example, of incitement to subversion, and of support to insurgency. . . . Our containment policy has, I believe, been wise and still remains necessary."[90] Moreover, as the scholars pointed out, "the potential threat of [China's] revolutionary aspirations for Asia . . . is now recognized by every non-Communist state in the region."

[87] *New York Times* (March 11, 1966).

[88] *Idem.*

[89] *New York Times* (December 20, 1967).

[90] Reischauer, *Beyond Vietnam,* pp. 161-63.

In spite of this division in serious scholarly opinion, John Kenneth Galbraith has commented in one of his articles, with the sort of superciliousness that has come to mark much of the critical literature, that Asians have "brainwashed" Americans about the threat of China by telling them what they want to hear.[91] Without any confirming evidence, Galbraith asserts that "all [those] familiar with the area *should* know this." But until writers such as Galbraith can offer evidence to the contrary, I, for one, remain more impressed by accounts like the following which reports on the recent meetings of the Association of Southeast Asian Nations (an association including Indonesia, Malaysia, Singapore, the Philippines and Thailand): "Fear of Communist China and its increasing hostility toward most governments in the area was a common impulse among the member nations. . . ."[92] And one is also impressed by the comments of Kenneth T. Young, who is an expert in Southeast Asian affairs, was President Kennedy's Ambassador to Thailand, and is President of the Asia Society: "Thailand has had forty years of the Communist Party supported by the Communist Chinese. Survival is their first national interest and they feel that the Communists are the greatest threat to their survival."[93] Whether or not these points of view are finally decisive, it is reasonable to assume that policy-makers would want to give them serious consideration.

C. *Expectations and Their Realization*

In one sense America's foreign policy in Asia is in a very

91 Galbraith, *op. cit.,* p. 132.

92 *New York Times* (August 18, 1967).

93 *New York Times* (May 7, 1967).

anomalous situation at present. At the very time when the U.S. is bogged down in an apparently interminable, costly and increasingly unpopular war, many of the general expectations U.S. policy has been engendering in Asia since 1945 are showing promise of being realized. As former Ambassador Edwin O. Reischauer has eloquently argued, ". . . time is on our side in Asia."[94] Japan has made striking progress and has become, rather than China, the wave of the future in Asia. South Korea has made vast economic strides and somewhat more limited political and social advances since 1961 when Syngman Rhee was ousted.[95] Malaysia has made very impressive progress in economic and political terms, and its general position is much strengthened by the overthrow of an aggressive Indonesian administration. Indonesia itself, after a revoltingly bloody transition, appears to be moving in a somewhat more progressive and sober direction than was the case under Sukarno.[96] The economic advance of both Thailand[97]

[94] "Time Is on Our Side in Asia," *Reader's Digest* (February, 1967).

[95] See Kim, *op. cit.*

[96] See Adam Malik, "Promise in Indonesia," *Foreign Affairs* (January, 1968). Note particularly the strong emphasis Malik puts upon regional cooperation in the form of ASEAN, pp. 301-303.

[97] It is difficult to know how to assess books like Louis E. Lomax's *Thailand: The War That Is and the War That Will Be* (New York, 1967), which is advertised as "a first-hand report of another Vietnam in the making." It is safe to say the book has not received enthusiastic support from those who know something about Thailand, although, I take it, the problems to which Lomax points are real ones. As of June 22, 1968, and the promulgation of that nation's new constitution, some of Lomax's charges about lack of constitution, voting, and open discussion of politics are no longer completely true; see *New York Times* (June 22, 1968). Assessment of these things is basically a matter of degree. While there is "visible evidence of a political

and Taiwan[98] is impressive, although both countries have yet much progress to make in political and social affairs.

In short, the spirit of "regional momentum," as we have called it, is beginning to manifest itself concretely in collective economic enterprises like the Association of Southeast Asian Nations, to which we have already called attention. This pattern of development is fully in line with the moral directives of the Truman Doctrine, and it is a pattern well worth encouraging.[99]

That is one side of the picture. On the other is a disheartening war where all hopes and expectations seem daily less capable of being fulfilled. Are we not manifestly contradicting ourselves in Vietnam by announcing great expectations about peace, pacification, self-determination, equality of economic and political opportunity, etc. and all the while pursuing a policy that "Americanizes," that "militarizes," that destroys the people, that props up a self-serving "Mandarin" military junta, that refuses to seek peace when the chance comes, and on and on? As we have mentioned, many critics believe our policy to be so transparently self-contradictory that anyone

awakening" in Thailand, there is still a long, long way to go. My own untutored judgment is that Lomax underrates the degree to which Thailand's future is contingent upon the settlement in Vietnam and (therefore) Laos; see the comments of various experts on "Thailand: The Northeast" in *Asia* (Fall, 1966), particularly those by David Wilson, p. 14.

[98] Neil H. Jacoby, "United States Aid and Taiwan's Economy," *Asia* (Fall, 1967).

[99] See ch. X, "The Far East in the Equation of Global Power," in George Ball, *op. cit.,* for a sensible and enlightened discussion of the current political and economic developments in Asia and of the proper U.S. response.

who defends it "must" be driven by unconscious or unconfessed motives of the most devious sort. I shall not attempt to settle the debate (for on a number of questions I am very uncertain myself), but I shall attempt to show that terms like "arrogance of power" illumine not at all the actual reasons behind policy decisions.

To begin, we must recall the nature of the threat to South Vietnam — and Southeast Asia — as President Kennedy conceived it, and the way he sought to confront the threat. Roger Hilsman reports that for Kennedy the fundamental problem in Vietnam was a socio-political one. Nevertheless, the solution had to be "orchestrated" with properly calibrated military operations. That is, what was needed was a carefully conceived counterinsurgency operation. And it is here that Sir Robert Thompson, the British counterinsurgency expert already mentioned, featured so prominently. For it is Sir Robert who is the "hero" of Hilsman's account and it is his ideas, so far as I can tell, that have continued to influence the recommendations of Kennedy exiles like Arthur Schlesinger, Jr., John Kenneth Galbraith and Richard Goodwin.

It is to the credit of Thompson, Hilsman and Armbruster, I believe, that they resist all temptation to sentimentalize guerrilla warfare. The amazing capacity of a relatively small number of armed terrorists to control an area and to "tie down" a vast number of regular forces should have become apparent to us out of our own experience with rioting in the summer of 1967, if it were not already apparent in Vietnam.[100]

[100] Hilsman, *op. cit.*, p. 429. For an exceedingly interesting elaboration of this point, see Armbruster, "Guerrilla Warfare and Vietnam: A Perspective," in Kahn, *et al, op. cit.*, pp. 92ff.

As Thompson points out, "The figures indicate that the insurgents' strengths . . . in both Malaya and Vietnam [until the end of 1964] were at no stage any more than one per cent of the population, and initially a good deal less than that. This does not qualify an insurgency as a 'People's Revolutionary War,' but only as a revolutionary form of warfare designed to enable a very small, ruthless minority to gain control over the people."[101]

Similarly, as our domestic summer experiences indicate, coercion represents no long-term solution to social disruption and dissatisfaction, although it obviously plays an indispensible role in dealing with the problem immediately. The long-term solution to the problem of insurgency is the task of pacification, or civic and political development. Thompson's pattern for implementing this sort of development — the "strategic hamlet" program — showed some signs of success by early 1962.[102] That is, the prospects of pacifying South Vietnam did not appear to be hopeless, although Thompson made it quite clear that the program would be long and hard, taking at least ten years, if not more, for completion. Above all, the whole operation demanded persistence and determination. If one were to "win" the war, this was the only way. But to a seasoned observer like Thompson — and Hilsman concurred — it was certainly worth a try.

Unfortunately, President Diem and his brother badly misunderstood the strategic hamlet program, and in '62-'63 they began rushing it and, consequently, ruined the program. The strategy needed to be carefully integrated into the building

101 Thompson, *op. cit.,* p. 49.

102 Hilsman, *op. cit.,* pp. 462-63.

of a central administration, and this did not happen. First Diem botched the plan, then he was overthrown and the successive governments during 1964 were so unstable as to afford no chance for progress in pacification.[103] This brought things to an unhappy pass at the beginning of 1965.

[103] In evaluating the realistic potentialities of the Strategic Hamlet Plan (as well as some current modifications of it, as in Kahn, *et al, op. cit.*—see below), one is again up against the irreducible fact of differences in expert opinion. Bernard Fall in *Viet-Nam Witness,* pp. 272-73, is very skeptical of the relevance of the entire strategy for Vietnam. The differences between Malaya, where the strategy was very successful, and Vietnam, are simply too great. In implying that people like Thompson were unaware of the differences, Fall is certainly in error; see Thompson, "A 10-to-20 Year War in South Vietnam?" *U.S. News and World Report* (February 13, 1967), p. 94. But whether Fall's skepticism is well-founded I am not competent to say. I am impressed with Duncanson's extensive description of the possibilities and failures of the plan as it was applied in South Vietnam (see Duncanson, *op. cit.,* pp. 311-27). Duncanson's judgment is worth considering: "Much had gone wrong in the implementation of the strategic-hamlet idea. Ngo Dinh Nhu expected the fences to bring victory over the Viet Cong without supporting measures, by moral force alone, provided the whole people underwent the same regime. . . . [But] there was nothing strategic about the siting of the hamlets, and the security forces were encouraged to pursue the Viet Cong kinetically, without bothering to consolidate the defense of the belt of hamlets; big unguarded gaps were left in between, and in the gaps even more of the isolated watchtowers and outposts were overrun— and weapons lost—than in the previous period. . . . In trying to cover the whole country in just over a year, the program exhausted everybody and left no work over to do the following year. . . . Yet if these faults could have been put right, the attitude of the peasants was evidence enough that they appreciated the intention to free them from the exactions of the Viet Cong and the crossfire of battle" (pp. 325-26). Much of Duncanson's analysis is related to his overall judgment that the failure of the regimes in South Vietnam was fundamentally a failure in judicious administration.

1965 is obviously the critical point in the case of Vietnam so far as many who dissent from U.S. policy are concerned. It was in the Spring of that year, with the bombing of the North in February and the intervention of combat troops in June, that many ended their support of President Johnson's policies. The President is accused of having misled the people in the '64 campaign, and I would agree that he should have done much more to prepare the people for the possibility of massive intervention.[104] Worse, he is accused of "Americanizing" and "militarizing" the struggle with very little reason and very little justification,[105] and of departing from concern for pacifi-

[104] I believe Sir Robert Thompson has summarized perfectly the dilemma Johnson found himself in in 1964 when, by all accounts, Allied prospects were fast becoming very dim: "No President in an election year could have committed combat troops on the scale required to prevent the situation deteriorating as it did throughout 1964." "Can the Vietcong Ever Win in Vietnam?" reprinted in the *New York Times* (September 10, 1967). As I indicate below, I think there was really very little choice open to the President on the question of the 1965 escalation, and yet one wishes Johnson might have begun to prepare the American public for the necessities of the situation. Had he done this, he would have forestalled much of the subsequent talk about a "credibility gap." Max Frankel, in "Why the Gap Between L.B.J. and the Nation?" *New York Times Magazine* (January 7, 1968), p. 44, claims that the reason Johnson "fuzzed" the 1965 escalation was his "overriding desire to avoid a provocation of the Soviet Union or Communist China." This may be; indeed it is quite plausible. Still, the Administration must get very low marks for "finding a middle way" between international and domestic political realities, on the one hand, and preparing the American public to cope with the unavoidabilities of a complex situation, on the other. This is part of the "communication problem" to which Frankel rightly points in his essay. Cf. Bill D. Moyers, "One Thing We Learned," *Foreign Affairs* (July, 1968).

[105] See Appendix B.

cation and civic action. This is Hilsman's objection (and the reason for his resignation from the government),[106] as well as of less circumspect defectors like Schlesinger and Goodwin. In effect, Johnson had "sold out to the Pentagon."

In the light of the bitter criticism that has mounted along these general lines since 1965, it is worthwhile to cite at length the observations of the chief architect of civic action and pacification in Vietnam. In 1966, Sir Robert wrote:

> By the beginning of 1965, the Viet Cong had established a position in South Vietnam whereby they were in control of large areas of the countryside and had sufficiently penetrated the towns to create conditions of instability, which, in turn, were undermining the whole fabric of organized government. . . . The two major threats which developed from the situation were, first, that the armed forces of South Vietnam might be defeated piecemeal and their morale broken, thereby destroying the physical base for continued resistance to the insurgent; and, second, that the government itself might completely collapse, thereby destroying any remaining political base. . . . Whereas in the past this aid may have been limited to a continual flow of small

[106]In a long footnote on pp. 531-32, Hilsman provides what is essentially his refutation of the reasons for bombing, and, in effect, he provides the reasons why he decided to leave the Administration. The best I can do, in trying to evaluate Hilsman's arguments, is to hold them alongside the arguments of Thompson, Pike, Honey and others (see below), who would not agree with Hilsman that "although things had not been going well . . . they were not yet so serious as to require such measures of desperation." With such conflict in judgment, it is not easy to make a conclusive evaluation on this one way or the other.

parties of men and materials, the insurgent movement will now be in a position to absorb whole regular units and heavier weapons. Secondly, as soon as it becomes apparent that there is a danger of escalation, others will become alarmed by the situation and pressures will develop to effect a ceasefire and to end the war by negotiations. This will not appeal either to the insurgent, who can see victory on the ground within his grasp, or to the government, for whom the prospect of negotiations from a position of absolute weakness might be the last straw in breaking the morale of its own forces and eroding its own position.

This is the moment of decision for the supporting power, to whom it will be quite clear that the alternatives are either an outright victory for the insurgent and the complete submersion of a people who have been fighting valiantly over the past few years for their freedom and independence, or its own major involvement in the fighting. I doubt whether any supporting power which has both the resources and the resolution could, in such circumstances, fail to choose the second alternative.[107]

[107] Thompson, *Defeating Communist Insurgency,* pp. 166-67. Cf. Thompson, "A 10-to-20 Year War in South Vietnam?" *U.S. News and World Report* (February 13, 1967): "Q. Do you favor an end to the bombing of the North?" "A. No, not at all. It has two useful purposes: First, if the bombing of infiltration routes and facilities continues, the North Vietnamese infiltrators walk into South Vietnam [and] that makes them a much easier proposition for the anti-Communist forces than they would be if they arrived in the South by truck.

"Secondly, I think the bombing is warranted as a way of making it clear to North Vietnam or anyone else that, if they commit aggression in one way, then they must expect a reply to it possibly in another

66

Thompson's words speak for themselves, and are echoed by Duncanson,[108] Honey,[109] Pike,[110] and others.[111] These reason-

way." "Q. Is the military campaign . . . a waste of lives and effort?" "A. That's not what I'm saying. . . . Before American combat troops went into action, the Viet Cong were about to win. I think they would have won in 1965. Resistance in South Vietnam would have collapsed if American combat forces had not gone in. . . ." Cf. Thompson, "Can the Vietcong Ever Win in Vietnam?" I wish to stress that in all of these sources Thompson is at the same time urging a "low-level, long-term" operation as the only strategy for winning. He has some very strong things to say about over-use of fire power (see below). Nevertheless, he sees the war in Vietnam in terms that are much less of the either/or variety than many of the critics, including the Kennedy exiles—*either* large-scale military action *or* pacification and counter-insurgency activity. Thompson implies that the relation between these things is a good deal subtler than is generally understood.

108 Duncanson, *op. cit.,* pp. 366-67.

109 Honey, *op. cit.,* pp. 31-32.

110 Pike, *op. cit.,* pp. 163-65. Pike speaks of the decision on the part of Hanoi and the N.L.F. to "militarize" the struggle in 1964. "The militarization of the effort, which included ordering thousands of North Vietnamese regular army soldiers to the South, had behind it various motives" (p. 164). Pike contends that among these motives was the certainty that victory was just around the corner and it was necessary just to make the final push. Pike's analysis here ought to be held over against Draper's arguments against escalating the war.

111 George Ball's discussion of Vietnam in *Discipline of Power* (pp. 293-343), which I find generally congenial, manifests a certain ambivalence on the matter of the start of bombing in 1965, although Ball became unqualifiedly opposed to the continuation of bombing (his book was published before the April, 1968 cut-back). On p. 321 Ball writes: "In my view, it was a mistake to start the bombing, although I understand very well the considerations that prompted the decision to begin—and all the issues were exposed to the full benefits of an adversary process [critics please take note!]. The bombing has, as I see it, seriously impaired the moral authority of the United States, increased our alienation from the other free nations, exacerbated

able, eminently qualified individuals make a very plausible case for the major escalation undertaken by Johnson in 1965. For the President to overlook the evidence cited by people of Thompson's caliber would, in my view, not only be "arrogant," but also "mindless." The people I have cited are, so far as I can tell, neither "militarists" nor "power-hungry." Certainly, if these individuals are taken seriously, it is much less easy to talk about clear distinctions between "their" war and "our" war.[112]

There is a persistent line of criticism that judges Johnson's major escalation in 1965 to have inaugurated a pattern of preference for fighting over negotiating. *The Politics of Escalation*[113] attempted to document this, and it is a line often enunciated by Schlesinger, Galbraith and others. U Thant's promises to support it have often been invoked to prove that the U.S. would rather fight than talk.[113a] Administration pro-

internal strains and fissures, and greatly increased the dangers of intervention by the big Communist powers. At the same time, I doubt that it has had much effect on the war in the South." Then, on p. 323, Ball indicates that he understands it is not so easy to stop, once the policy was begun. But even more, he is willing to concede "that the air offensive [may have] usefully served a temporary purpose [during the dire times of 1965] and that now we should be concentrating in the South where the issue must ultimately be decided."

[112] If these people are right, things came to such a state in 1964 that "their war" was desperately contingent upon "our effort." It was not because Johnson was lusting either to Americanize or to militarize the war, but because the country was about to be overrun. To accept that under existing conditions would, I believe, have been a very grim choice indeed.

[113] Franz Schurmann, Peter Dale Scott, Reginald Zelnik, *Politics of Escalation* (New York, 1968).

[113a] In April, 1968, David Kraslow and Stuart H. Loory published

tests that Hanoi and the N.L.F. have no serious interest in working out a fair and peaceful accommodation were generally dismissed. Even after the substantial cut-back in U.S. bombing of the North and the beginning of preliminary talks in Paris, one still heard that the U.S. bore the major responsibility for impeding the success of the talks.[114] (The Reverend

a series in the Los Angeles *Times* entitled "The Secret Search for Peace in Vietnam," which was soon expanded into a book by the same title (New York, 1968). Although I have read only the *Times* reports, there is an important difference between the kind of criticism they make and that of the authors of *Politics of Escalation*. In the latter book, opportunities for talks are said to have been missed because of an unrelenting desire on the part of the Johnson Administration to escalate the war. For Kraslow and Loory, missed opportunities are much more the result of inadvertence and bad coordination (though some of the evidence they supply shows that Hanoi was not falling over itself to get to the peace table). Generally, I am more convinced by Kraslow and Loory than by Schurmann *et al.;* however, I am sure one of the reasons the U.S. did not want to talk in '64-65 was that it was then in a position of extreme weakness. There seems little doubt that the U.S. and the South Vietnamese government are in a relatively stronger bargaining position now than in '64-65. Of course the Administration is to be held responsible for negligence but, morally speaking, the charge of negligence is not so severe as that of deliberate contrariness. Nevertheless, one of the truly disturbing aspects of this war has been the continuing presence of inadvertence (rightly documented by Schlesinger in *Bitter Heritage* and by David Halberstam in *Making of a Quagmire*). That it keeps on recurring is difficult to understand, despite the undeniable complexities of the situation. At least one of "the lessons of Vietnam" lies in the direction of correcting this sort of mindlessness.

[114] Since the peace talks began in Paris, much of the wind has been taken out of the sails of the moderate critics, such as the late Senator Robert Kennedy and other Kennedy Administration exiles. The main lines of the recommendations made by Senator Kennedy—reduction in Northern bombing and peace talks—have certainly gone a long

William Sloane Coffin, Jr. received a standing ovation at Yale Divinity School in April, 1968, for saying, among other things, that President Johnson most likely did not want talks and was dragging his feet on the matter of a site so as to minimize the chances for success. Then he could say that, well, he had tried and with new gusto get back to escalating.)

Given the difficulties of knowing the mind of the government, this line of argument had always been hard to prove or disprove. Over against it there is a great deal of contradictory opinion — some of it very carefully documented — from Max Frankel, Thompson, Duncanson, Hoang Van Chi, Herman Kahn and his associates, Pike and Reischauer.[115] In this view, the attitudes and dispositions of North Vietnam and the N.L.F. are more responsible for the obstacles to negotiation than the U.S. government. Duncanson cites several statements by North Vietnamese leaders which are nothing but a "cynical approach to the process of negotiating a peace."

> Fighting while negotiating is aimed at opening another front, at making the puppet army more disintegrated, at stimulating and developing the enemy's contradictions and thereby depriving him of propaganda weapons [that is to say, so that he can no longer point to Communist intransi-

way towards being met. See R. F. Kennedy, *To Seek a Newer World* (New York, 1967), pp. 205-228, and Theodore C. Sorenson, "The War in Vietnam: How We Can End It," *Saturday Review* (October 21, 1967).

[115] See Max Frankel, "How Long Will It Last?" *New York Times Magazine* (April, 1967); Thompson, *op. cit.,* p. 94; Duncanson, *op. cit.,* p. 374; Hoang Van Chi, "Why No Peace in Vietnam?" *Vietnam Seen from East and West,* pp. 44-45; Kahn, *et al, op. cit.,* pp. 50ff.; Pike, *op. cit.,* pp. 360ff.; Reischauer, *Beyond Vietnam,* p. 8.

gence as the obstacle to peace], isolating him further, and making those who misunderstood the Americans see clearly their nature. . . . Whether or not war will resume after the conclusion of agreements depends on the balance of forces; if we are capable of dominating the adversary, war will not break out again, and the converse also holds true.[116]

Now that serious negotiations appear to be getting underway in Paris, the U.S. public seems pacified, to a degree. In the long run, whether the talks will be of more value than this, and who it is that will be proved right about them, will depend upon their end result. That is, we shall finally be able to assess the real value of the talks only in the light of an evaluation of what kind of settlement is achieved.

In my judgment, if one considers the expectations raised by the U.S. with regard to the future of South Vietnam, then any negotiated settlement which satisfies all the desires of the North Vietnamese and the N.L.F. to dominate South Vietnam as well as "the components of former French Indochina" (in Lacouture's words),[117] would be an inescapably disturbing prospect.[118] As the late Robert Kennedy put it, not long before he died, "our investment in Vietnam, not only in lives and resources, but also in the public pledges of Presidents and leaders, is immense. . . . Simply to surrender it, to cancel pledges and write off lives, must raise serious questions about what other investments, pledges and interests might similarly be written off in the face of danger or inconvenience."[119]

116 Duncanson, *op. cit.,* p. 374.

117 See fn. 79 above.

118 See Ball, *op. cit.,* p. 311.

119 Kennedy, *op. cit.,* p. 118.

Whether or not this argument is finally conclusive, I do not see how any thoughtful person can ignore it, or fail to weigh it carefully.

It may be, of course, that there is finally no acceptable alternative to negotiating a face-saving withdrawal for Allied forces, and to making a major concession to North Vietnamese and Chinese interests in the area. Perhaps, as the critics keep saying, the cost in lives, effort, demoralization and diversion of resources is too high and we must choose this alternative.[120] But, on the strength of the considerations we have reviewed, a policy-maker who reached that decision could only do so in deep anguish, much as a decision to carry on must be anguishingly made.

Certainly, in light of the Tet offensives,[121] the continued

[120] See, e.g., R. M. Brown, *op. cit.,* pp. 75-76; Mary McCarthy, *Vietnam* (New York, 1967); Zinn, *op. cit.,* ch. 6. Also Sheehan, *op. cit.* All of the observations that these individuals make about the horrors of the war are terrifying. It is in cataloging these things that the critics undoubtedly make their greatest impact upon sensitive people. Except for Sheehan, it is in discussing the other aspects of the Vietnam conflict that these authors are so much less persuasive or, let us say, are far more self-confident than they ought to be. They are, consequently, of little help to those who try to weigh and balance a number of conflicting considerations.

[121] There is new evidence that, according to their own estimates, the Viet Cong and North Vietnam did not accomplish what they set out to accomplish in the Tet offensives, even though they obviously won a number of important goals. According to a captured document, "We failed to seize a number of primary objectives . . . to hold the occupied areas . . . to motivate the people to stage uprisings. . . . The enemy still resisted and his units were not disrupted into pieces. . . . We cannot achieve total victory in a short period." Cited in Dennis Warner, "Vietnam: Hard Battles Still to Be Fought," *Reporter* (May

resiliency of the Viet Cong and the North Vietnamese forces, and the instability of the South Vietnamese government, the overriding question put by Kahn and his associates, "Can we win in Vietnam?" becomes all the more urgent. If, as critics like Richard Barnet contend,[122] the U.S. can under no

2, 1968). See also Herman Kahn, "If Negotiations Fail," and Samuel P. Huntington, "The Bases of Accommodation," in *Foreign Affairs* (July, 1968) for discussions of the Tet offensives.

The same assessment was made in a recent and rather encouraging dispatch in the *New York Times* (January 3, 1969): "Major Gains Made by Vietnam Allies, Even Critics Assert." If (and this is a big "if") the appraisal is correct—e.g., that "no more than 15 per cent of the population [un]willingly supports the Viet Cong"—it is very significant. Furthermore, the dispatch indicates that the political leadership of the Viet Cong was seriously weakened by the Tet offensives. The spirit of this report contrasts sharply with two pre-Tet dispatches in the *New York Times* at the turn of 1968: "U.S. Report Finds Gloom in Vietnam" (December 5, 1967); "U.S. Said to Press Sharply for Good Vietnam Reports" (January 1, 1968).

122 Richard J. Barnet, "The Last Act in Vietnam," *New York Times Magazine* (February 4, 1968). One's confidence in Barnet's general assessment of the war would be greater were it not for an unbecoming self-confidence about aspects of the war that are a good deal more doubtful than Barnet allows. Barnet's premise for what amounts to the unilateral withdrawal of U.S. troops is that the war is basically *internal* to South Vietnam and that the N.L.F. is basically "moderate" in its aims and eager to cooperate with other nationalist groups within the South. I have already said enough in this paper to argue for the doubtfulness of Barnet's views. But he should certainly realize that these views *are* arguable and that if one does not hold his sanguine outlook about the goals and probable methods of the North Vietnamese and N.L.F., one would be far less happy about accepting his solution. I believe that William Pfaff's observations are relevant to people of Barnet's persuasion: "It may be noted that even many of . . . those on the New Left who frankly sympathize with the N.L.F., often will argue that a Communist victory would produce an essentially liberal solution to the crisis. Their position is that the U.S. is

73

circumstances "win" its final objective of preventing the North Vietnamese and the N.L.F. from controlling South Vietnam, or if Reischauer's latest judgment is true, that we have already and completely lost the counterinsurgency war, then it makes no sense to keep pursuing a policy that pretends we can win.[123]
wrong to oppose the N.L.F. because the N.L.F. will create a society in Vietnam substantially in accord with 'true' American ideals, with land reform, a liberated peasantry, and popular government. Thus they, too, might be said to be American believers in 'victory'—in this case a victory of American values over 'reactionary' policy pursued by the present American Government. What they do not concede is that a Communist victory in Vietnam might create a repressive and anti-liberal society, that reprisals and militant ideological indoctrinations of an unwilling population might take place, that a Communist government might prove itself quite as capable of despotism and cruelty as any of the non-Communist regimes of the last fiteen years. They, too, cannot allow themselves to imagine 'defeat.' " Kahn, *et al, op. cit.,* pp. 166-67. This, it must be remembered, comes from one who is himself very critical of U.S. policy in Vietnam.

The depressing, but hard-headed article by David Halberstam, "Return to Vietnam," *Harper's* (December, 1967) is, I take it, more in line with the suggestions of Pfaff, namely, that the outlook of losing is not pleasant but that we simply cannot win in any sense of the word. Alas, even Halberstam's solution—"encouraging our Vietnamese to talk to their Vietnamese"—is not precise.

[123] Edwin O. Reischauer, "A Broad Look at Our Asian Policy," *New York Times Magazine* (March 10, 1968). Obviously, this essay was written during the panic of the Tet offensives, when it appeared that all was lost. These offensives were simply more than Reischauer's always very precarious support of Administration policy could bear. Aside from some sharp inconsistencies between what he argues in *Beyond Vietnam* and in "A Broad Look" (especially on the question of the repercussions for the area of a Communist victory in South Vietnam), the main difficulty with this article is its unstated conclusion that we have no alternative but to get out and move back to "firmer ground." All the really hard questions of how we move from

But even if people like Barnet and Reischauer are right, the question of a standard of victory (and defeat) is still relevant. Although we may not win in any accepted sense of the term, it is still important to know how badly, or to what degree, we must lose. That is, it is important to know what kind of settlement we can actually obtain, well short of our optimum expectations. William Pfaff, a more thoughtful critic than most, understands this point well: "If my pessimistic view of the war is accepted, the conclusion must be that our choice is not . . . between ways to obtain a success of some recognizable kind, but between *ways of limiting defeat.*"[124] In short, no matter what our situation in Vietnam at the present time, we desperately need what Kahn calls a "generally accepted and reasonably valid" "theory of victory" against which we can measure our accomplishments and failures as well as define some realistic expectations.

Among those generally sympathetic with the U.S. cause in Vietnam, there is a fairly widespread rejection of the existing theory of victory held by the U.S. military — what Kahn calls the "attrition-pressure-ouch" theory.[125] Kahn lists the following reasons why this theory is most unlikely to succeed:

A to B in South Vietnam are, unfortunately, ignored. Reischauer may be guilty of forgetting his own wise counsel in *Beyond Vietnam:* "One can understand the desire to conserve American strength for more constructive tasks than this unhappy war. We are all eager to save American lives and end the carnage in Vietnam. But it is possible that in our eagerness to do this we might help produce such instability in Asia and such impotence in ourselves that the development of a more stable, prosperous, and peaceful Asia might be delayed by decades" (p. 15).

124 Pfaff, *op. cit.,* p. 168; italics added.

125 Kahn, *op. cit.,* pp. 181ff.

1. Will power and commitment of V.C. and North Vietnamese leaders were and are probably too strong.

2. Costs were not — and will not be — raised high enough to affect the enemy's will power significantly. Perhaps more important, the tactics of escalation were almost inherently ineffective.

3. Not enough attrition could — or can — be achieved to weaken decisively the enemy's capabilities in the short run, even though enough may be achieved to limit the enemy's efforts.

4. There is too much pressure for quick and demonstrable results for any "last fifteen minutes" theories of victory to be politically acceptable.

5. North Vietnamese and N.L.F. adjusted their theory of victory and tactics to take into account the change in the situation once the U.S. introduced large combat forces into South Vietnam and began to offer a plausible counter to U.S. "attrition-pressure-ouch" theory of victory.[126]

The objective underlying present U.S. policy — basically, to get the North Vietnamese and the N.L.F. to cry "uncle" — explains in great part the reliance on heavy weaponry and conventional strategy. (Kahn points out that not until *1967* did the South Vietnamese forces begin to receive intensive anti-guerrilla training. [127]) The use of this weaponry and strategy has been disturbingly portrayed in Frank Harvey's *Air War—Vietnam*[128] and strongly emphasized in *In the Name of America*.[129]

[126] *Ibid.*, p. 195.
[127] *Ibid.*, p. 60.
[128] (New York, 1968).

Thompson echoes the criticisms of Harvey, Kahn and many other thoughtful observers when he writes:

It staggers belief that American helicopters were under instruction, and for all I know still are, to fire on any village which fires on them in the course of their flight (I am not here referring to an opposed landing but a few passing shots). This return fire reinforces every word the Viet Cong say, with the result that American intentions cease to be credible. It is this sort of thoughtless direct response reaction, where lives are not even at stake, which is helping to prolong, if not lose, the war. . . . The emotional argument, that anything which saves the life of one American boy is permissible, will in the long run waste the deaths of many more. The rule of law and the maintenance of the highest standards are prerequisites to the creation of the right image, which is vital both in South Vietnam and in relation to the grand strategy.[130]

129 Director of Research, Seymour Melman. Published by Clergy and Laymen Concerned About Vietnam, 1968. It seems to me that Paul Ramsey, in an unpublished critical review of this volume, has discovered its basic flaws: "The reader is repeatedly told that these are not legal judgments, and that he must try to avoid thinking they are. At the same time, categorical legal judgments are affirmed throughout; they are as 'formal' as verdicts of illegality could possibly be, except that the sponsors and compilers of this volume do not constitute a legal tribunal." See also the review by James Finn in *The New Republic* (June 1, 1968), for conclusions more or less the same as Ramsey's. Finn's criticisms are actually more interesting since he is a good deal more sympathetic to the "spirit" of the document than Ramsey. I would agree with Finn that *In the Name of America* catalogues some very disturbing incidents, incidents which, as Robert Thompson indicates below, often work against the purposes for which the war is being fought.

In rejecting the prevailing theory, observers such as **Kahn**, Armbruster, Gastil, Thompson, Duncanson and Lansdale[130a] would most certainly not agree with Barnet and Reischauer's assessment that we have already lost the war. And even if they did, they would still (with Pfaff) feel it imperative to work out scenarios for *limiting defeat*. Thus, unlike Barnet and Reischauer and so many other critics, they would develop in any case *careful strategic and tactical plans for guiding Allied military and political activity*. These individuals all wisely recognize Duncanson's indisputable dictum: "At the stage now reached, non-intervention is itself a form of intervention — the withholding of support as positive a pressure as increasing it: in the Vietnam conflict there is no longer a neutral position."[131]

What these observers understand so much better than most wholesale critics of the war is that even a negotiated settlement is going to be determined *not* primarily by what takes place in Paris, but by what takes place in Vietnam (and in the United States!). We and our allies, just as the Communists have done, must set for ourselves *some* reasonable objectives — some theory of victory — and resolutely pursue it.

The theory of victory and the attendant strategy recommended by Kahn, Thompson, etc. have always struck me as plausible but, as yet, essentially untried. They are based on Bernard Fall's (and Thompson's and Duncanson's) percep-

130 Robert Thompson, "Squaring the Error," *Foreign Affairs* (April, 1968), p. 453.

130a See Edward G. Lansdale, "Still the Search for Goals," *Foreign Affairs* (October, 1968), pp. 94-95.

131 Duncanson, *op. cit.,* p. 1.

tion that this is an "administrative war" — "the side with superior administration is likely to win."[132] In short, this is a scenario for gradually and systematically extending the administrative capacity (the capacity, among other things, to insure law and order) on the part of the South Vietnamese government. In Kahn's words, there is a

> . . . necessity of being able to demonstrate to supporters, critics and active opponents of our policies that we do have a plausible theory of victory that is being successfully implemented. . . . If, for example, there were a reasonable technique for creating secure areas in South Vietnam surrounded by a "frontier," if the military and pacification program for creating and enlarging such frontiers could be fitted into some systematic over-all plan and schedule, and, finally, if this plan and schedule could be demonstrated persuasively to a skeptical and even hostile audience, then an important dent might be made in the attitude of the critics.[133]

The technique, as worked out in impressive detail by Kahn, Gastil and Armbruster, is essentially a variation of themes conceived by Robert Thompson, themes, as Thompson describes them, which are "strategically defensive, for the offensive lies in the nation-building and the pacification" (or the building of administration).[134]

132 Kahn, *op. cit.,* p. 179.

133 *Ibid.,* p. 203. Cf. Duncanson, *op. cit.,* pp. 325-26.

134 See Thompson, *Defeating Communist Insurgency,* p. 450; cf. esp., Armbruster, "A Military and Police Security Program for South Vietnam," and Gastil, "Force Deployment and Control for a National Defense System," in Kahn, *et al, op. cit.,* chs. 7 and 8.

In my view, this theory of victory has much to recommend it, although there are some problems with it, such as those posed by George Ball.[135] The main difficulty is the matter of leaving inland, rural areas, at least initially, outside the "frontier."[136] As Ball says: "To abandon the inland areas we now hold would require us either to carry out a mass transfer of population or leave to the untender mercies of the Viet Cong large numbers of South Vietnamese who have helped our side."[137] In face of this and other problems, Ball sees no course but to carry on roughly along present lines. I am not sure Ball's objections are finally irreconcilable with Kahn's theory of victory. But a good deal of exploration is needed here.

There are also more pessimistic theories of victory (or defeat) that ought to be examined. I have in mind Pfaff's "federal" theory,[138] which is essentially the same as the one recommended by the Ripon Society in their paper, "The Realities of Vietnam: An Alternative for Republicans."[139] It is also like the proposal put forward by Huntington,[140] Shaplen,[141] and by the so-called "Tuyen Plan," reported on

135 See Ball, *op. cit.,* pp. 326ff.

136 This problem struck me as I pondered Gastil's strategic map. (Gastil, *op. cit.,* p. 301.) It is true, however, that he makes allowances for inland defense areas at places like Pleiku, Ban Me Thuot, Da Lat, and so on. Perhaps the problems Ball raises could be solved in somewhat the same way.

137 Ball, *op. cit.,* p. 327.

138 Pfaff, *op. cit.,* pp. 165ff.

139 *The Ripon Forum* (September, 1967).

140 Huntington, *op. cit.,* pp. 653ff.

141 "Vietnam: Crisis of Decision."

recently by Dennis Warner.[142] With some variations, all of these recommend local negotiating procedures by which Viet Cong and non-Viet Cong would work out a *modus vivendi* from region to region. In Pfaff's interpretation, all of these local arrangements would be represented in some kind of overall South Vietnamese coalition government which would be designed to prevent a complete Communist takeover for at least five years. Pfaff is, I must say, refreshingly honest about the prospects for this plan: "A pessimist about the war, I am also a pessimist about peace. . . . [This plan] is not one I think it very likely we can achieve."[143] His suspicions are reinforced by Dennis Warner: "If the goals of the N.L.F. and those of Hanoi were primarily the restoration of peace on honorable terms, then the prospects of negotiations along Tuyen's lines might be reasonably bright. Unfortunately, however, the proposition seems highly improbable."[144]

Finally, there is always the "enclave" solution as yet another middle way. However, with the possible exceptions of Galbraith[145] and Senator Eugene McCarthy,[146] most people,

142 Warner, *op. cit.*

143 Pfaff, *op. cit.,* p. 167.

144 Warner, *op. cit.,* p. 17.

145 Galbraith, *op. cit.*

146 Senator McCarthy proposed General Gavin's "enclave policy" in *The Limits of Power* (New York, 1967), p. 195, and implied his support at a later date; see *New York Times* (June 14, 1968), p. 32. Aside from McCarthy's rather generalized protests against the war, it was difficult to locate a detailed and carefully elaborated discussion of his views on Vietnam. The Senator raised his "moral" objections to the war, and his campaign speeches stressed over and over the same

including apparently its alleged originator, General Gavin,[147] do not entertain it seriously any longer. The reasons why this proposal has lost ground are fairly obvious. Ever since the North Vietnamese bombardments of Con Thien and Khe Sanh, and, more recently, the bombardments of Saigon, it is clear that enclaves would be "sitting ducks" for endless rounds of devastating rocket harassment. Such enclaves promise no stable, confident way of life for anyone concerned. They would be entirely defensive operations — in the psychological as well

point. By turning to *The Limits of Power* I had hoped to find, at the least, the kind of fairly extensive treatment of Vietnam one finds in such books as Ball's *Discipline of Power* (50 pp.) or even Senator Kennedy's *To Seek a Newer World* (60 pp.). Shockingly enough, there are but nine pages devoted to the subject, written in an almost off-hand manner. This is not reassuring to those of us looking for informed leadership on matters of the utmost complexity and subtlety. Without some very careful explanation of what is meant by the enclave policy and some cogent defense of the strategy, it is difficult to muster much enthusiasm for the hasty recommendations McCarthy makes in his book.

[147] General Gavin's relation to the "enclave theory" is a bit strange. In a 1967 "Face the Nation" interview he reported that present strategy in South Vietnam is perfectly in accord with what he meant by the enclave notion! He also rejects the idea that by using the term "enclave" he meant a geographically static holding strategy (see *Vietnam Hearings,* p. 79). If this is true, those who advance the enclave idea ought to take note, for in debate the enclave notion has been used as an alternative to present policy. I must say that Gavin's words in "A Communication on Vietnam," *Harper's* (February, 1966) do not seem to support his more recent interpretation: "Today we have sufficient force in South Vietnam to hold several enclaves on the coast, where sea and air power can be made fully effective. By enclaves I suggest Camranh Bay, Danang, and similar areas where American bases are being established" (pp. 16-18). I am not sure Gavin has always been clear on just what he has meant by the term.

as the military sense of the word.[148]

However one stands on these complicated strategic and tactical questions, it is clear that sorting out and reflecting on specific theories of victory (or theories of realistic expectation) is the level at which *helpful* discussion goes on. Most important of all, when one plunges into discussions of this sort, he quickly comes to realize what we have been at pains to demonstrate throughout this paper: that our predicament in Vietnam is exceedingly complex and problematic, no matter how sensitive one is morally. It is no place for the disillusioned liberal.

We have contended, then, that with the formulation of the Truman Doctrine, the U.S. cultivated a set of hopes among the peoples of Asia for social and economic development within a reasonably reliable international framework. Most important of all, the U.S. sowed these seeds not simply with verbal promises but by itself becoming *an Asian power* — by laying itself on the line in World War II and after. That is, crucial decisions were made in the '40's and early '50's which very concretely linked the destinies of the United States with a vast number of Asian peoples. In the face of the available options, these decisions seemed not only wise but also *right;* they were in accord with the fundamental moral values of the American creed. Without necessarily subscribing to Dulles' extreme formulations, thoughtful Americans in the early 1950's, when Vietnam policy was initiated, generally did not question the motives of the U.S. in "desiring only the health of a new nation, and its sufficient strength to ward off the

[148] In some of his criticisms of an "active defense" strategy, Ball (*op. cit.*, p. 327) seems to have the enclave theory in mind.

83

Communist peril," as Reinhold Niebuhr put it. Many today would question the wisdom of the series of decisions that led to our specific involvement in Vietnam — and well they might.[149] But the decisions *were* made, international expectations were unquestionably developed *by our concrete presence,* and our responsibility for the lives and prospects not only of a substantial portion of the South Vietnamese people but for the lives and prospects of the peoples in neighboring countries *became a fact of life.*

As the cases of China and Indonesia make clear, the U.S. has not intervened militarily in the affairs of every Asian country "going Communist." But it is quite a different matter in Korea and Vietnam (as it would be, too, in West Germany) when the United States *is* involved and patterns have been established,[150] and when the failure of our government to act militarily would pose an awesome threat to the very existence of great numbers of people,[151] as well as "create regional in-

[149] Reischauer, *Beyond Vietnam,* pp. 20ff.

[150] It is, of course, the fact of concrete involvement in Vietnam that distinguishes that case from, say, the question of U.S. involvement in Hungary in 1956, or the Russian decision regarding its missiles in Cuba in 1962. The element of time and established expectations is crucial here. Russia had not, *over a period of time,* learned to live with the U.S. influence in Hungary, nor had the U.S. over a period of time learned to live with Russian missiles in Cuba. Both situations involved possibly drastic alterations in existing international expectations. In Vietnam it was the Communists who were attempting to make the drastic alterations.

[151] Herman Kahn estimates that were the North Vietnamese and N.L.F. to take over South Vietnam tomorrow, purges would run into the millions. *Can We Win in Vietnam?* p. 31; cf. "If Negotiations Fail," pp. 627ff. While it is difficult to be certain how he knows this, the following comment bears pondering: "Earlier this year in the city

stability of expanding proportions."[152] When the U.S. has, over a period of ten or so years, "lived out" a pattern of assurances against threats of this kind, it is not so much a loss of face that will result from giving in but, as Professor Reischauer rightly says, "a loss of faith." It may well be that the U.S. and Southeast Asia must eventually accept the serious consequences of an admission that the sort of expectations envisioned cannot be realized, or can only be realized at too high a cost for all concerned. But such a decision would be surrounded by moral as well as strategic ambiguity of an irreducible sort.

of Hue, the Viet Cong and North Vietnamese forces assassinated more than a thousand people, most of whose names were on prepared lists. How we would feel about the possibility of the Hue atrocities being repeated on a nationwide scale is a matter that does not need elaboration." "If Negotiations Fail," p. 628.

Nor is one at all reassured by the pattern of assassinations in the North after Ho Chi Minh commenced his Land Reform. Though it is difficult to get accurate statistics on this matter, Gerard Tongas, a French professor and eye-witness, writes: "This indescribable butchery resulted in one hundred thousand deaths." Tongas, *L'enfer communiste au nord Viet-Nam,* p. 222.

[152] Cited in Oberdorfer, "Noninterventionism, 1967 Style," p. 112.

III. CONCLUSION

The following words of Robert Osgood are, I believe, extremely pertinent in articulating what we have been driving at throughout this paper:

> Unless Americans constantly relate their pursuit of national security and national interest to a hierarchy of universal values, they will, ultimately, drive out of their national, as well as their international conduct, those moral qualities which are as indispensable to national welfare as character is to personal welfare. . . . Because the United States is unavoidably thrust into a position of global leadership, her standards of conduct must, inevitably, have a great influence in setting *the moral tone* of international relations in general. Consequently, it behooves Americans to conduct its foreign relations in a way that will encourage the kind of international environment compatible with its ideals and interests.[153]

Osgood is claiming, in effect, that the "national interest" of the United States both *is* and *ought to be* defined with reference to explicit moral values. As we suggested earlier, the fundamental "moral qualities" of American life are not ethnic

[153] Osgood, *op. cit.,* pp. 444, 450; italics added.

or nationalistic in character; the Declaration of Independence does not say "all *American* men are created equal. . . ." Consequently, Osgood concludes, the United States cannot logically attend to its own "national welfare" without at the same time attending to the welfare of "all men." As he very rightly states at another point, "If the . . . values which are the basis for America's social and political institutions *are valid at all, they are as valid outside American borders as within.*"[154] That is, I repeat, a logical judgment — given the universalistic character of American values. It is not simply Osgood's sentimental opinion.

Understood in this way, America's concern for an "international environment compatible with its ideals and interests" is a necessary extension of its peculiar national interest, namely, one that is defined in relation to a universalistic moral creed. If it is to be true to its ideals, the United States must hope to create what Wolfers calls "milieu goals," or conditions that establish a favorable climate for the cultivation of the values the United States holds dear.

Now we would join Osgood in arguing against one of the expressed tenets of the tradition of liberal disillusionment: that moral claims in the international realm *always* mask base forms of self-seeking. Or, as Hans Morgenthau has put it, ". . . the invocation of moral principles for the support of national policies is *always and of necessity* a pretense. . . ."[155] On the contrary, we have been arguing that in the Far East, for example, the development of the Truman Doctrine was a

154 *Ibid.*, p. 125.

155 Good, *op. cit.*, p. 278; italics added.

87

very complicated mixture of concern for national survival and economic interest and genuine moral concern for, the welfare of the people of Japan, South Korea, the Philippines, and so on. Furthermore, the Truman Doctrine engendered expectations that the United States, at some cost to itself, intended to encourage "regional momentum" in the direction of participational societies.

We argued further that in the Far East generally, and Vietnam specifically, the case is *by no means clear,* as the critics claim, that under the cover of high-sounding moralism the U.S. is massively undermining the hopes for progressive political and economic development in the region. We attempted to show that it is at least plausible to believe that the Administration is not lying or "snowing" the public when it contends: (1) that there is now regional momentum in Asia and Southeast Asia that is worth protecting and encouraging, and that a substantial portion of these countries believe it to be worth protecting and encouraging; (2) that there is a substantial portion of the South Vietnamese population which does not desire subjugation to a North Vietnam-Viet Cong Communist government; and (3) that some pattern of military response has been necessary if these considerations are to be honored.

One may, of course, finally dissent from each or any of these points. But *the case must be argued* against that body of reasonable and informed opinion which offers varying degrees of support for the Administration's interpretation. It simply will not do — to cite one example — for critics like Fulbright, McGovern, Draper, Niebuhr, etc. to beg all sorts of questions by baldly asserting, as though it were obvious, that the Vietnam war is nothing but a "civil war" in which the U.S. is arbitrarily intervening. Such may be the case, but it *has to be demonstrated at length* and with utmost care in face of a good deal of serious legal and historical argument to the contrary.

We have suggested that, in general, foreign policy decisions create patterns of expectations, expectations which, in the case of the United States at least, are infused with moral significance. To affirm the American moral creed is to adopt a point of view that makes it logically impossible to come to decisions exclusively on the basis of whether they contribute to the interests of the United States. The benefit of Americans is bound up with the benefit of "all men." For this reason, representatives of that good American tradition — the tradition of liberal disillusionment — could never consistently be morally cynical in matters of international affairs. Consciously or not, they would have to concern themselves with those means which produce "the freedom and independence of all," in Kennan's favorite words. This tradition concludes, simply put, that "keeping one's own house in order" *is* the most effective way to produce a "better world" for all.

We cannot say that the so-called Wilsonian strain is "moralistic" in viewing foreign affairs and the tradition of liberal disillusionment is not. Both are morally sensitive along very much the same lines, for both are chips off the same block. The only serious difference arises over instrumental matters, over whether intervention or non-intervention is, as a rule, the most efficient means for attaining the shared end.

Now the liberals of the '20's and '30's became disillusioned precisely because of their passionate "moralism" — which they never lost. Not only did the "great expectations" embodied in Wilsonianism remain unfulfilled, many of Wilson's actual policy decisions clearly worked against the realization of the desired freedom and independence for all. That is, the obvious internal conflict between announced moral expectations and actual decisions was itself the source of the intense liberal criticism of Wilson's policies. Disillusionment gave rise to the generalization that moral rhetoric in foreign affairs is bound to be a pretense of some sort.

But the members of this tradition were not sufficiently reserved in their conclusions. Something like the following would have been fair enough: In *some* foreign policy situations moral rhetoric can be used to cloak devious motives and self-seeking objectives. Admittedly, such a maxim loses much of the homiletic power that one finds in the expressions of Charles Beard, George Kennan or Senator Fulbright. Yet this maxim seems a good deal closer to the truth, possibly because it looks suspiciously like common sense.

The primary virtue of this maxim — as opposed to the stronger, more absolute one of the disillusioned liberals — is that it does not presuppose the very thing that must be examined, namely, how and to what extent moral justifications do or do not hide "lower" motives and objectives. To adopt our maxim is to move rather modestly from situation to situation without predispositions about how moral considerations and other considerations "must" relate to each other. One would expect to find hypocrisy in some circumstances and a mixture of honest moral conviction and self-seeking of various kinds in other circumstances. In short, without prejudgments about the relation of moral rhetoric and foreign policy decisions, one will be free to examine in depth and with care the actual situation — the conditions surrounding it as well as the consequences which are likely to result from it.

I have attempted to do exactly that in the case study of Vietnam. I would not wish to draw large conclusions from the study about the relation of moral expectations and other considerations in foreign policy decisions. What is true in Vietnam may well be untrue of decisions made with respect to South Africa or Latin America. (My approach leaves other situations quite open for further investigation.) But *in the particular situation of Vietnam* I do mean to question what appear to be the doctrinaire judgments of many prominent individuals who so obviously stand in the tradition of liberal disillusionment. And I do mean to argue that while the expectations of U.S. foreign policy in Asia need constant review and reappraisal, and serious mistakes and miscalculations need to be prevented, these expectations are not a mask for some demonic purpose, nor are they fundamentally alien to the aspirations of great numbers of people who inhabit that area of the world.

It may be that because of the excessive costs of our Vietnam policy and because of the fragmented and inherently unstable conditions of South Vietnam, we and our allies will have to settle for something rather "less than expected." However, given the state of affairs in Southeast Asia — present possibilities and potentialities — the decisions regarding a settlement in Vietnam *really are hard decisions,* involving the reconciliation of a number of relatively imponderable moral and political claims. To admit this is not, of course, to relieve the Administration of the burden of acting responsibly in Vietnam. Nor is it to withhold criticism regarding the manner in which aspects of our policy have been conceived and implemented. But it is to recognize that in making the inevitable decisions, those in charge are more to be pitied than censured.

APPENDIX A

The Problem of Aggression in the Vietnam War

It is obvious that a central point of contention in the debate over Vietnam is the question of whether "aggression" has been committed. Much of the controversy surrounding many aspects of the war hangs on this matter. Since most of the critics of U.S. involvement seem to accept the proposition that evidence of aggression would point to a dangerous infringement of international order, they are at pains to show that no such evidence exists. We might, of course, devote several pages simply to documenting and detailing the discussion about aggression carried on by various critics, but most of their arguments can be condensed into one basic argument: that the struggle in Vietnam is a "civil war" and not a war that involves the arbitrary crossing of an internationally recognized territorial boundary and the initiation of an armed attack. Senator Fulbright's comments may be taken as representative: "It is said that we are fighting against North Vietnam's aggression rather than its ideology and that the 'other side' has only to 'stop doing what it is doing' in order to restore peace. But what are the North Vietnamese doing, except participating in a civil war, not in a foreign country but on the other side of a demarcation line from two sectors of the same country. . . . What are they doing that is different from what the American North did to the American South a hundred years ago. . .?" (Fulbright, *op. cit.,* p. 107; cf. Kennan, *Vietnam Hearings,* pp. 143-45; Zinn, *op. cit.,* pp. 72-82; Draper, *op. cit.,* chap. 5, pp. 149-52; Oglesby, *op. cit.,* pp. 11ff.; Lawyers Committee Statement, *op. cit.;* Senator George McGovern, "Lessons of Vietnam," pp. 4ff.)

Several things are usually implied by the use of the term "civil war" and they must be sorted out. First, because the Vietnam conflict is assumed to be a war "between geographical sections or political factions of the same nation," it is concluded that the word "aggression" has no relevance. Second, because it is a civil war, outside countries, such as the U.S., have no right to intervene. Third, regardless of the relationship between North and South Vietnam the question of aggression is particularly irrelevant because "it is a civil conflict *within* South Vietnam," as Kennan says. (*op. cit.,* p. 145.)

While we cannot hope to settle these very complicated questions, we can raise some plausible objections to the standard contentions of the critics. We shall do this in four steps, which, it seems, cover most of the salient aspects of the problem. Anyone reflecting on the matter will have to come to terms with each of these four issues.

1. In the light of the Korean experience, it is not clear that the matter of "aggression" is irrelevant even if it can be shown that a conflict involves two geographical sections of the same country. In a sense the Korean War was a civil war. The 38th parallel was an arbitrary and artificial

line of demarcation that had absolutely no political or social meaning in the history of Korea, nor was it intended as a permanent dividing line. Despite these facts, the U.N. Security Council adjudged the 38th parallel to be an internationally recognized territorial division with respect to which "aggression" by the North against the South became an *international* offense.

That the Security Council authorized U.S. action by virtue of a diplomatic blunder on the part of Russia should not obscure certain important aspects of the Korean case. As Spanier points out, "the logical assumption that the United States would not have responded to the Communist challenge in Korea if the Soviet Union had been present at the council table does not follow. . . . If the Soviet Union had been present at the council table and cast a veto, the Western powers would probably have invoked Article 51 [as the U.S. has done in Vietnam], which allows for the individual and collective self-defense of United Nations members in case of U.N. inaction. . . . Prime Minister Clement Attlee suggested this very possibility . . . on July 5, 1950." (Spanier, *op. cit.,* p. 38.) Even though the Korean Republic was not a member of the U.N., Attlee's application of Article 51 seems fully in accord with the general interpretation of the Article. As the McDougal Brief points out, "Apparently no international law scholar has ever seriously suggested that the U.N. Charter prohibits the right of self-defense of non-members" (p. 59). In short, there seems nothing offensive about applying Article 51 to one part of a country that is provisionally separated from another part of the same country, even though that part of the country is not a member of the U.N. (See also, Hull and

Novogrod, *op. cit.,* pp. 125ff.)

2. What argues against the civil war interpretation with respect to Vietnam is that the dividing lines (38th parallel in Korea, 17th parallel in Vietnam) in both Korea and Vietnam *were international constructions* in the first place; these lines, by definition, involved the interests and expectations of a community of nations, not simply of the particular nations themselves. In this sense, there is obviously no analogy whatsoever to the conditions surrounding the American Civil War.

This brings us, of course, to the tortured problem of the Geneva Accords—precisely what they assured and what they did not. And here precision is perhaps impossible to achieve. Because of explicit reservations neither the U.S. nor South Vietnam signed the Accords, and *no* nation signed the crucial Final Declaration (providing for elections, temporary partition, etc.). The diplomatic status of an unsigned document is uncertain. What is more, the Accords were simply a very ambiguous set of arrangements. Hilsman summarizes them well: "On balance the loopholes which riddled the Geneva agreements favored the Communists. The lack of rules for the I.C.C. created endless opportunities for the Communist member, Poland, to obstruct and confuse its activities, and the requirement that all I.C.C. decisions had to be unanimous made it possible to paralyze them. There were no provisions for creating the necessary conditions for free and fair elections in Vietnam. . . ." (Hilsman, *op. cit.,* p. 104.)

For further elaboration of the ambiguities of the Accords, one ought also to consult the essays by John Norton Moore, in Falk, *op. cit.* In my judgment, Falk's response to Moore's analysis of the Accords is not only weak but misleading. Falk says: "It would consume too much space to refute Moore's interpretation of the Geneva Accords on a point-by-point basis especially as this task has already been done effectively by other authors" (p. 465). These "other authors" turn out to be Kahin and Lewis, who are not lawyers and whose book is singularly lacking in careful legal analysis, and Donald Lancaster. This is what Lancaster has to say about the Accords: "The Armistice Agreements, which had been hastily drawn up in order to comply with Mendes-France's self-imposed time-limit, were carelessly drafted, and in the case of Vietnam the validity of the agreement itself was open to question since it had been negotiated and signed by representatives of the Commander-in-Chief of the French Union Forces in Indochina, in spite of the protests of the Saigon Government which, as the authority charged with the civil administration of the southern zone, would be responsible for the execution of some of its provisions." (Lancaster, *op. cit.,* p. 338.) It would be hard to imagine a sloppier use of sources than Falk's references to Lancaster. (Cf. Duncanson's treatment which is similar to Lancaster's, *op. cit.,* p. 204.)

When discussing the Accords, two points must be touched on: (a) the question of elections and, (b) the question of the international status of North and South Vietnam.

(a) Though this is a murky question, I find myself in agreement with the judgment of Hull and Novogrod, as well as with that of Ball. Hull and Novogrod state: "It would appear that South Vietnam, as a result of its treaty with France, was bound to accept the Accords [including provisions to enter into consultation on elections], but that the U.S. was not obliged to do so [not having signed the Accords].

97

Second, it would seem that the election provision, despite the contrary views of Washington and Saigon, was of significance." (Hull and Novogrod, *op. cit.,* p. 50.) And Ball remarks that Dulles should have coerced Diem to enter into consultations. Because he did not, "we have been embarrassed . . . ever since in defending the legal position of South Vietnam. Mr. Dulles was a man of experience and astuteness and, as a well-trained lawyer, knew well the advantages of forcing the adversary to make the procedural mistakes. I find it curious, therefore, that he did not press Diem more vigorously to live up to the procedural requirements of the Accords. Because North Vietnam was a police state *there were demonstrable reasons why elections were out of the question* and this could have been vividly shown to the world had Diem only been persuaded to attend the consultations." (Ball, *op. cit.,* p. 338; italics added.)

In short, as Ball understands, there could never have been any elections, but it was important to have placed the onus of failure on the heads of the North Vietnamese, not on the heads of the South and the U.S. — where it has fallen in world opinion. (The reasons why there could have been no elections are clear: "In 1955 the Americans were given to understand in no uncertain terms that there were not going to be any free [U.N. supervised] elections in North Vietnam, North Korea or East Germany," wrote Kenneth T. Young in *Asia* [Winter, 1966], p. 121.)

But, as Hull and Novogrod point out, while the failure to enter into consultations weakened the case of the South and the U.S., "North Vietnam was not justified in employing force against the South when it discovered that the elections would not be held. To conclude otherwise would be to deny the well-established rule that force may only be employed in self-defense. . . ." (This point about the use of force in self-defense makes unpersuasive a familiar claim — that South Vietnam's procedural violations of the Accords justified the North's action. See Falk, *op. cit.,* p. 264.) The general conclusion the two authors come to regarding the Accords is also worth citing: "The ease with which Hanoi and Saigon can substantiate their legal positions, the impotence of the Control Commission, and the ostensible limited nature of the Accords lead the astute observer to conclude that the Geneva Accords, by themselves, cannot be dispositive of the legal issues arising out of the Vietnam conflict. . . . It might very well be concluded that to unravel the legal issues emanating from the Vietnam struggle, one must direct his attention to the larger body of general international and organizational law" (pp. 50-51).

(b) B.S.N. Murti, in his *Vietnam Divided* (New York, 1964), summarizes well the international status of North and South Vietnam: "Since the Geneva Accords two independent sovereign states, claiming sovereignty over the whole country, came into existence in Vietnam and the division of the country seems permanent. . . . Both the States are completely independent with fullfledged Governments of their own owing no allegiance to the other" (p. 176). South Vietnam has by now been recognized as an independent state by about sixty nations, and it has twice nearly been admitted to the U.N. "The history of the U.N. resolutions and debates on the status of the two Vietnams after the 1954 Geneva Accords leaves no doubt that the Republic of Vietnam is recognized as an independent state under international law and some of the debates lend support to the proposition that there are now two independent states in Vietnam." (McDougal Brief, p. 28.)

Furthermore, as Kahin and Lewis point out in their otherwise critical volume, the SEATO Treaty was signed in the clear recognition that South Vietnam, as a "protocol state," was an independent state (pp. 62-63). The Treaty was agreed to in September, 1954 by eight nations — Australia, France, New Zealand, Pakistan, the Philippines, Thailand, the United Kingdom and the United States — and not by seven states as Richard Goodwin says in *Triumph of Tragedy* (New York, 1966, p. 111), or as Senator Fulbright says in his book, (p. 110). Both men should know better. (We deal with the status of the SEATO Treaty in relation to U.S. action in Appendix B.)

3. But even if, in two steps, a reasonable case can be made that the 17th parallel did come to have a great deal more international significance than the critics admit, it is still necessary to show that some sort of "armed attack" took place in order to prove that the term "aggression" is relevant to the Vietnam situation. Again, the issues here are almost as cloudy as in the case of the Accords, although, be it noted, to understand this is a gain for the discussion. If nothing else it would modify the sometimes incredible self-assurance that issues from the critics.

I do not believe that the Johnson Administration manifested nearly enough subtlety on this question. By talking about "armed aggression from the North" (as, for example, in the State Department White Paper, *Aggression from the North,* 1965), and by likening Ho Chi Minh to Hitler (who, in any man's language, was obviously guilty of "armed attack"), the Administration laid itself open to attacks like those of I. F. Stone. A much more promising tack was that taken by President Kennedy and Roger Hilsman in using terms like "concealed aggression." There is a good deal of reasonably impartial evidence for this; for example, Theodore Blockley, a Canadian Legal Advisor to the I.C.C., was writing in reports to the Canadian government as early as 1957: "The mounting intensity of North Vietnamese sabotage, subversion and guerrilla operations in South Vietnam, and the apparent inability of the Commission to inhibit *this attack,* raise the very real possibility that defensive measures undertaken by the South Vietnamese government may include . . . calling upon the U.S. for assistance." (italics added.)

On March 30, 1961, a SEATO report, unanimously endorsed, "noted with concern the efforts of an armed minority, again supported from the outside. . . ." (Brief, p. 36.)

There is, of course, the well-known affirmation issued by the I.C.C. on June 2, 1962: "There is evidence to show that the [North Vietnamese] have allowed the Zone in the North to be used for inciting, encouraging and supporting hostile activities in the Zone in the South, *aimed at the overthrow of the Administration in the South."* Even more interesting is the report published by the Canadian member of the I.C.C. Legal Committee on February 13, 1965: "[The hostile activities of North Vietnam] are in direct and grave violation of the Geneva Agreement, and *constitute the root cause of general instability in Vietnam.* . . . The cessation of hostile activities by North Vietnam is *a prerequisite to the restoration of peace in Vietnam as foreseen by the participants of the Geneva*

101

Conference of 1954." (Brief, p. 35; italics added.)

Incidentally, Zinn (*op. cit.,* pp. 75, 78) cites articles by David Halberstam to disprove the "aggression theory." It is perhaps noteworthy that Halberstam says, in his previously mentioned *Harper's* essay: "I think the evidence is more complete than ever that Hanoi has controlled this war since 1957 . . ." (p. 48).

Several critics have implied that if the North was indeed infiltrating and subverting it was Diem who started it by parachuting his agents into the North; see, e.g., Noam Chomsky, "Intolerable Evils Justify Civil Disobedience," *New York Times Magazine* (November 26, 1967), p. 27. Duncanson's comment is relevant here: "D.R.V. complaints later on, on the activities of sabotage teams from the R.V.N., were probably well founded, but these amounted to no more than nuisance reprisals for acts of terrorism inspired by the North in the South." (Duncanson, *op. cit.,* fn. a, p. 225.)

A good deal more could be made of the traditional "armed attack" notion with respect to North Vietnam's activity in Laos. Since the late 1950's at least, the North has had regulars fighting alongside the Pathet Lao. (See Hilsman, *op. cit.,* p. 91. See also Bernard Fall, "The Pathet Lao," in *The Communist Revolution in Asia,* ed. Robert A. Scalapino, Englewood Cliffs, N. J., 1965). By late '67 the North had an estimated 50,000 regulars against the Souvanna Phouma neutralist government; see Charles Mohr, "Laos, Thailand and War," *New York Times* (October 10, 1967).

So far as Vietnam is concerned, what status can one give to "concealed aggression" in relation to Article 51 of the United Nations Charter? Does such activity constitute "armed attack"? Suffice it to say that many U.N. declarations and a good deal of international legal opinion suggest that it does. In 1950, for example, the General Assembly "solemnly reaffirms that whatever the weapons used, any aggression, whether committed openly or by *fomenting* civil strife in the interest of a foreign power or otherwise, is the gravest of all crimes against peace and security throughout the world." (Brief, p. 43.) More directly, Professor Hans Kelsen writes: "Since the Charter of the United Nations does not define the term 'armed attack' used in Article 51, the members of the United Nations in exercising their right of 'individual or collective self-defense' may interpret 'armed' attack to mean not only an action in which a state uses its armed forces but also a revolutionary movement which takes place in one state but which is initiated or supported by another state. In this case the members could come to the assistance of the legitimate government against which the revolutionary movement is directed." (Quoted in Brief, p. 49.) See also the excellent discussion of the general problem of aggression in "Resort to Coercion: Aggression and Self-Defense in Policy Perspective," ch. 3 in McDougal and Feliciano, *Law and Minimum World Public Order* (New Haven, 1961).

4. One of Draper's favorite arguments is that the Johnson Administration radically changed its position on aggression in 1965. Prior to that year it was supposed to have called the Vietnam conflict a "civil war." But when the Administration needed to escalate its justifications along with its military escalation (a popular charge), it started talking about "aggression." (See pp. 88f. and 150.) Insofar as one keeps in mind the kind of "concealed aggression" we have been talking

about, this contention is extremely doubtful, to say the least. President Kennedy's allusions to aggression as early as 1961 have already been mentioned. And Rusk was talking about subversion from the outside as early as November, 1961. (See *Teach-Ins: U.S.A.,* p. 201.) Perhaps most significant of all is W.W. Rostow's very important speech in June, 1961: "It is important that the world become clear in mind . . . that the operation run from Hanoi against Vietnam is as clear a form of aggression as the violation of the 38th parallel by the North Korean armies in June, 1950." (*Viet-Nam Reader,* p. 113.) See Hilsman's account of the Taylor-Rostow mission to Vietnam in 1961 which produced the same conclusions.

APPENDIX B

The Problem of Justification for Direct U.S. Military Involvement in Vietnam

The problem of justification for the 1965 escalation is yet another amazingly involved problem or set of problems. We must touch on two aspects, (a) the SEATO Treaty and (b) the Gulf of Tonkin Resolution.

(a) It would appear that very injudicious things have been said on all sides with regard to the SEATO Treaty. Richard Goodwin (*op. cit.*, pp. 18ff.) is right, I believe, in criticizing the Johnson Administration for somewhat belatedly stressing the "binding" quality of the Treaty as it affects military action in Vietnam. At best, Goodwin says, the Treaty is permissive (see Brief, p. 62, for a summary of its significance). But then, in the interest of not overrating the Treaty, he makes a curious statement which probably underrates it. (Draper, too, seeks to reduce the Treaty's significance to nothing; see pp. 156-68.) Goodwin writes: "One can search the many statements of Presidents and diplomats [prior to 1965] in vain for any mention of the SEATO Treaty" (p. 19). I say this is curious because it is not difficult to find frequent references to SEATO in very important contexts prior to 1965. It is strange, for example, that the critics ignore the Joint Declaration issued by Presidents Eisenhower and Diem in 1957. (Draper examines only Eisenhower's well-known letter to Diem of October 23, 1954.) "Noting that the Republic of Vietnam is covered by Article IV of the Southeast Asia Collective Defense Treaty, President Eisenhower and President Ngo Dinh Diem agreed that aggression or subversion threatening the political independence of the Republic of Vietnam would be considered as endangering peace and stability." And the very important statement by President Kennedy on March 23, 1961, regarding Laos: "If these attacks by externally supported Communists, namely North Vietnam, do not stop, those who support a truly neutral Laos will have to consider their response. The shape of this necessary response will, of course, be carefully considered, not only here in Washington, but in the SEATO Conference with our allies. . . ." (Hilsman, *op. cit.,* p. 91. Hilsman adds: "The implication was war.")

Then, too, there is the Gulf of Tonkin Resolution itself (see below). "Consonant with the Constitution of the U.S. and the Charter of the United Nations and in accordance with its obligations under the Southeast Asia Collective Defense Treaty, the U.S. is, therefore, prepared, as the President determines, to take all necessary steps, including the use of armed force, to assist any member or protocol state of the Southeast Asia Collective Defense Treaty requesting assistance in defense of its freedom." As we are coming more and more to appreciate, the Gulf of Tonkin Resolution was not an incidental document.

Critics such as Don R. and Arthur Larson (*Viet-Nam Reader,* pp. 102-108) question whether unilateral action is

106

in fact permitted under Article IV of the Treaty. They are not persuasive about the language of the Article itself. Nor is legal opinion clear on this: "Ruth Lawson notes that under both the SEATO and NATO treaties '. . . the commitment to act in the event of an armed attack is a matter for unilateral decision. . . .' " (Brief, fn. 210, p. 192.)

Furthermore, while one would not wish to overrate the present status of the SEATO organization (it is virtually defunct from the point of view of France and Pakistan, and the United Kingdom is hardly an enthusiastic member), nevertheless five out of the eight member nations are involved in the Vietnam war. Australia has provided 8,200 troops; the Philippines, 2,000; New Zealand, 300-400; Thailand, 10,000. The United States and South Vietnamese contingents, together with the South Korean force (ca. 50,000), provide, of course, the bulk of the manpower. (The comparative involvement between the United States and allies in the Korean War, it may be noted, was in about the same proportions. "Even in 1950, there was, in the actual implementation of policy, no whole-hearted acceptance of the collective security principle. Small amounts of aid were given by a minority of nations other than the principal combatants; but ninety per cent of the forces engaged were either Korean or American." (Perkins, *op. cit.*, p. 107.)

In sum, the decision to intervene directly in Vietnam in 1965 was based on a wide range of strategic and political considerations (see Goodwin, pp. 16-32) and not strictly on the SEATO Treaty. However, the Treaty would appear to permit the decision. (It must also be remembered that in 1954 the U.S. made quite explicit that "it would view any renewal of the aggression in violation of the aforesaid Agreements with grave concern and as seriously threatening international peace and security." See Brief, pp. 73ff.)

(b) In one sense, the public debate about the Gulf of Tonkin Resolution is very odd indeed. The Congress explicitly stated that "the Resolution may be terminated . . . by concurrent resolution of Congress." So complex are the specific details surrounding the events that led up to the Resolution in August, 1964 (many of the reports are Classified), it seems incredible that ordinary citizens can claim competence to pass judgment. That is quite specifically the job of Congress. If the Administration was lying about the details, as many critics allege, then one hopes the Congress will simply repeal the Gulf of Tonkin Resolution, as it most certainly has the power to do. I am not persuaded by Senator Fulbright's remark that such a move is "no option at all" because "it would surely be interpreted as a repudiation of the President's leadership." (*The Arrogance of Power,* p. 51.) I do not have the impression that Senator Fulbright, or Senators like McCarthy and McGovern, have been overly embarrassed by appearing to repudiate the President's leadership! (Representative Lester Wolff began gathering votes to repeal the Gulf of Tonkin Resolution early in 1968. When President Johnson withdrew from the campaign and announced a cut-back in bombing, Wolff gave up his effort. While the prospects were never good for the success of Wolff's move, it was, nevertheless, the only really appropriate action for Congressional critics to take.)

Actually, Senator Fulbright is misleading the reader when he states that while the Resolution does give "Congressional endorsement for the conduct of a large-scale war in Asia" (which it certainly does — see below), "the resolution was adopted during an election campaign in which the President was telling the American people that it would be a mistake for the United States to become involved in a major war in Asia. . ." (p. 52). The Senator neglects altogether, for example, to discuss his concurrence in the 88-3 Senate vote of a pertinent appropriations resolution on May 6, 1965 (well after the election, and also after the beginning of bombing in the North in February, 1965). The President went out of his way to give Congress a chance to "show that [it] feels the same way today as it did last year when it passed the joint resolution urging the President of the United States to take whatever action he believes necessary in the interest of international peace in Southeast Asia. . . ." (As reported by Senator Saltonstall; see Brief, p. 110.) Certainly, the dissenting Senators — Gruening, Morse and Nelson — so understood it.

As to the Senate's awareness of the degree of discretion the Resolution granted the President, the debate surrounding the Resolution speaks for itself. Senator Fulbright argues (p. 52) that the debate was "perfunctory" and marked by "little deliberation." I have no doubt the debate could have been more extensive and enlightened, but the Senators were not without an appreciation of what was being determined in August, 1967, nor were they, as we have mentioned, in subsequent related deliberations.

The following discussion is most revealing. (Quoted in the McDougal Brief, pp. 101-106.)

Senator Fulbright, the Chairman of the Senate Foreign

Relations Committee who managed the resolution on the floor, said:

Mr. President, I recommend the prompt and overwhelming endorsement of the resolution now before the Senate. . . . The resolution further expresses the approval and support of the Congress for the determination of the President to take such action as may be necessary, now and in the future, to restrain or repel Communist aggression in Southeast Asia;

and it was said in a dialogue between Senators Brewster and Fulbright:

Mr. Brewster. . . . My question is whether there is anything in the resolution which would authorize or recommend or approve the landing of large American armies in Vietnam or in China.

Mr. Fulbright. There is nothing in the resolution, as I read it, that contemplates it. I agree with the Senator that that is the last thing we would want to do. However, the language of the resolution would not prevent it. It would authorize whatever the Commander in Chief feels is necessary. It does not restrain the Executive from doing it. Whether or not that should ever be done is a matter of wisdom under the circumstances that exist at the particular time it is contemplated. . . .

and in a dialogue between Senators Scott and Fulbright:

Mr. Scott. I support the resolution. I was glad to hear the chairman say that there is nothing in the resolution which limits the right of the President to repel any attack or prevent further aggression within the areas decribed in the resolution.

Mr. Fulbright. That is correct;

and in a dialogue between Senators Cooper and Fulbright:

Mr. Cooper. . . . Does the Senator consider that in enacting this resolution we are satisfying that requirement . . . of Article IV of the Southeast Asia Collective Defense Treaty? In other words, are we now giving the President advance authority to take whatever action he may deem necessary respecting South Vietnam and its defense, or with respect to the defense of any other country included in the treaty?

Mr. Fulbright. I think that is correct.

Mr. Cooper. Then, looking ahead, if the President decided that it was necessary to use such force as could lead into war, we will give that authority by this resolution?

Mr. Fulbright. That is the way I would interpret it. If a situation later developed in which we thought the approval should be withdrawn, it could be withdrawn by concurrent resolution. . . .

Mr. Cooper. I ask these questions because it is well for the country and all of us to know what is being undertaken. . . .

Under section 2, are we now providing the President, if he determines it necessary, the authority to attack cities and ports in North Vietnam, not primarily to prevent an attack upon our forces but, as he might see fit, to prevent any further aggression against South Vietnam?

Mr. Fulbright. One of the reasons for the procedure provided in this joint resolution, and also in the Formosa and Middle East instances, is in response, let us say, to

111

the new developments in the field of warfare. In the old days, when war usually resulted from a formal declaration of war — and that is what the Founding Fathers contemplated when they included that provision in the Constitution — there was time in which to act. Things moved slowly, and things could be seen developing. Congress could participate in that way.

Under modern conditions of warfare — and I have tried to describe them, including the way the Second World War developed — it is necessary to anticipate what may occur. Things move so rapidly that this is the way in which we must respond to the new developments. That is why this provision is necessary or important. Does the Senator agree with me that this is so?

Mr. Cooper. Yes, warfare today is different. Time is of the essence. But the power provided the President in section 2 is great.

Mr. Fulbright. This provision is intended to give clearance to the President to use his discretion. We all hope and believe that the President will not use this discretion arbitrarily or irresponsibly. We know that he is accustomed to consulting with the Joint Chiefs of Staff and with congressional leaders. But he does not have to do that.

and Senator Kuchel said:

I remember the Middle East resolution. I remember the Formosa resolution. Both came to Congress from President Eisenhower. Both were requested so that all might know that the people's representatives in this branch of the Government agreed with the Chief Executive of the United States with respect to the authority he possessed and the circumstances under which he would be compelled to utilize his power. . . .

That is the plain intent of the joint resolution now about to be passed by Congress. . . .

and Senator Cooper said:

In response to my questions, the distinguished Chairman of the Foreign Relations Committee, the Senator from Arkansas [Mr. Fulbright], and I believe, the chairman of the Armed Services Committee, the Senator from Georgia [Mr. Russell], confirmed my viewpoint that in passing this joint resolution we would satisfy the conditions of the SEATO treaty, and would exercise our constitutional function to give the President of the United States authority to do what he determines may be proper and necessary with respect to any situation which affects our security in South Vietnam.

I believe that is the essence of the second section. At least that was the meaning and interpretation given to it by the chairman of the Foreign Relations Committee;

and Senator Thurmond said:

The resolution which we are considering today does approve a new element which has not, prior to this week, been exercised, and that is the taking of all necessary measures to prevent further aggression. I sincerely hope that the President will take all necessary measures to prevent further aggression, not only against our own military forces, but also to prevent further aggression against our Southeast Asian allies. . . .

and Senator Morse who opposed the resolution among other

113

reasons on the ground that it was an unconstitutional "pre-dated declaration of war" said:

Another Senator thought, in the early part of the debate, that this course would not broaden the power of the President to engage in a land war if he decided that he wanted to apply the resolution in that way.

That Senator was taking great consolation in the then held belief that, if he voted for the resolution, it would give no authority to the President to send many troops into Asia. I am sure he was quite disappointed to finally learn, because it took a little time to get the matter cleared, that the resolution places no restriction on the President in that respect. If he is still in doubt, let him read the language on page 2, lines 3 to 6, and page 2, lines 11 to 17. The first reads:

The Congress approves and supports the determination of the President, as Commander in Chief, to take all necessary measures to repel any armed attack against the forces of the United States and to prevent further aggression.

It does not say he is limited in regard to the sending of ground forces. It does not limit that authority. That is why I have called it a predated declaration of war, in clear violation of Article I, section 8 of the Constitution, which vests the power to declare war in the Congress, and not in the President.

What is proposed is to authorize the President of the United States, without a declaration of war, to commit acts of war. . . ;

and:

No one can read the joint resolution and the authority proposed to be given the President in the joint resolution without recognizing that it would clearly authorize the President to proceed to follow whatever courses of action are necessary in his opinion; and such action would constitute authority to conduct war. . . ;

and in a dialogue between Senators Gruening and Morse, both of whom opposed the resolution, it was said:

Mr. Gruening. This resolution, in effect, is an authorization which would be the equivalent of a declaration of war by the Congress. Would it not be?

Mr. Morse. I think so.

Mr. Gruening. That is one thing I am very apprehensive about. If we should get into an all-out war, which I fear may happen, this resolution would be considered the authorization by the Congress to so proceed. Would it not?

Mr. Morse. That is correct;

and Senator Morse said:

Under the resolution Congress would give to the President of the United States great authority, without coming to the Congress and obtaining approval by way of a declaration of war, to carry on a land war in South Vietnam. The choice is left up to him. . . .

and Senator Gruening said:

This resolution . . . not only endorses all our Government has done to date in Southeast Asia, but also gives the President a blank check not merely to do whatever he likes in South Vietnam, but, to quote the text of the resolution:

> To take all necessary steps, including the use of armed force, to assist any member or protocol state of the Southeast Asia Collective Defense Treaty requesting assistance in defense of its freedom.
>
> That is, in effect, a predated declaration of war, if and when the Executive chooses, and war not merely in South Vietnam but in all Southeast Asia. . . .

(See Hull and Novogrod, *op. cit.,* pp. 169-80, for an excellent discussion of the legal status as well as the meaning of the Gulf of Tonkin Resolution. In this section the authors provide several reasons *against* superceding the Gulf of Tonkin Resolution with a formal declaration of war. Basically, their reasons come to this: It is virtually impossible to fight a limited war on the basis of a formal declaration, given the prevailing understanding of declarations of war in the international community. A declaration is taken to mean all-out war. See especially p. 175.)

A good deal of surprise was expressed when it became known that drafts of the Gulf of Tonkin Resolution were actually ready before the Tonkin incidents that took place in early August, 1964. (See, e.g., *New York Times,* December 22, 1967.) But one's surprise could last only until one had read the Resolution. The first paragraph mentions the naval attacks. The second paragraph states: "Whereas these attacks are part of a deliberate and systematic campaign of aggression that the Communist regime in North Vietnam has been waging against its neighbors and the nations joined with them in the collective defense of their freedom. . . ." Obviously, it was not the naval attacks as such that were the primary concern of the U.S. but the wider pattern of "concealed aggression"

116

that had been going on for at least five years and was becoming progressively more serious. The rest of the Resolution makes this perfectly clear. Thus the Tonkin incidents (if they in fact occurred) were but an open manifestation of a much broader and more serious threat that had been present for some time, a threat that had, however, remained generally hidden. The U.S. felt it needed an open provocation in order to respond as many felt it had to, if South Vietnam was not to be overrun.

Designed and Printed by Woodhaven Press, N. Y.